Demystifying Postgraduate Research

To Andrea and Louis for their love, support and patience

Demystifying Postgraduate Research

From MA to PhD

Jonathan Grix

THE UNIVERSITY
OF BIRMINGHAM

UNIVERSITY PRESS

Copyright © University of Birmingham Press 2001

First published in the United Kingdom by The University of Birmingham Press, Edgbaston, Birmingham, BI5 2TT, UK.

ISBN 1-902459-35-0

British Library Cataloguing in Publication data
A CIP catalogue record for this book is available from the
British Library

Printed in Great Britain by MPG Books Limited, Bodmin. Cornwall
Typeset by Book Production Services, London,

Contents

List of figures

Preface

The idea for the course from which this book took its inspiration originated over several beers in a pub in Birmingham. My drinking companion, Charlie Jeffery, and myself discussed introducing an intensive induction course for postgraduates in our institute. Since that time a number of people have contributed to shaping the thoughts in this book in a variety of different ways. Before thanking them, I wish to highlight the driving force behind the pages that follow. Whilst we all know the old cliché, 'knowledge is power', it is worth reflecting on the ways in which knowledge is discussed, disputed and disseminated. In the social sciences there are a number of different 'discourses' between disciplines, for example, economics and cultural studies. Common to most discourses is the basic language of research. It is my contention that in order to be able to work within the parameters of social science, you need to be very clear about what the tools and terminology of research are and what they mean *before* you can begin researching. If you spend a little time learning the language of research, learning what the terms and concepts mean and how they can be employed, the mystery associated with much of postgraduate work, especially the doctorate, will begin to disappear.

I would like to thank Willie Paterson, or 'boss' as he is known, for the numerous pleasant discussions we have had on several aspects of the book. Above all, I would like to thank him for his help with the sections on the viva and on publishing to which he contributed, verbally, to a considerable degree. Willie, Paul Cooke, Colin Hay, and Charlie Jeffery and Paul Cooke were kind enough to read an entire draft manuscript for me and to offer me many sound comments and pearls of wisdom. Ben Rosamond and Frank Webster were very generous with their time, read huge chunks of manuscript and provided me with excellent feedback and support, all of which influenced the final text. Lyn Brydon, Beth Edginton, Dan Hough and Ben Shepherd read sections of the manuscript for me and furnished me with welcomed comments and suggestions.

In addition, I would like to thank all the students on the induction course for their invaluable feedback and suggestions for improvement. In particular, David Mayo deserves a mention for the energy with which he supplied me with, and readily discussed, reading material and texts on specific areas dealt with in this book. Claire Suggit proved an excellent researcher, as she scoured the university library for material to help with the glossary of terms and definitions. Thank you too, to colleagues who contributed to the induction course, in particular Bill Dodd, Steve French, Lothar Funk, Adrian Hyde-Price, Charlie Jeffery, Kerry Longhurst and Wilfried van der Will. A special thanks to Nadia Haberman for putting the draft manuscripts together.

I have been fortunate enough to have an excellent working relationship with my editor, Alec McAulay. The sessions we have had discussing this book and other projects have been very enjoyable and peppered with good humour and professional insight (on his part). I am particularly grateful to Alec for his comments and suggestions for the sections on publishing and writing a thesis. I would also like to thank the anonymous reviewer whose insights and suggestions for improvement were gratefully received and frequently acted upon.

Finally, thanks to my wife, Andrea, who suffered my unbounded enthusiasm in a great number of discussions on matters dealt with in this volume.

August 2001

Introduction

The purpose of this slim volume is clear from its title. It is to equip students with some of the most important tools and terminology of research and, moreover, with an understanding of these terms. If you command the basic vocabulary of generic research, you are far more likely to choose the correct theories, concepts or methods to use in your work. By grasping the core tools used in research, much of the mystery that can surround it begins to disappear. This book *does not* give you in-depth expositions into the crucial debates or use of methods in social science research. I am interested in clarifying the terms and terminology associated with research – that is, any research, whatever discipline within the social sciences – and offer an introductory, and, hopefully, thought-provoking discussion on some of the key issues in research. The book is thus generic and non-disciplinary: that is, it takes a step back from disciplines and their assumptions and presents the tools common to most social research.

Throughout this book there are a number of recurring tensions. They can be summed up as the following:

- excellent scholarship versus pragmatism (or time constraints)
- the extent to which a researcher should interact with empirical data using preconceived ideas, hunches, categories or assumptions
- the extent to which ideas, hunches, categories or assumptions should arise from the data themselves
- research methods and the ontological and epistemological underpinnings invested in, and associated with, them by researchers.

The first three points above are related and I believe that they can be overcome. Time is *not* a guarantee for good scholarship, but knowledge of the 'nuts and bolts' that make it up can go a long way to ensuring that the tools of research are used properly. If you have the right tools and you know how to employ them, the research process becomes a great deal easier and *quicker*. Given the temporal constraints of doctoral research, and the fact that a researcher needs some sort of guide to their pursuit of knowledge, *some form of preconceived idea, notion or hunch* is essential to begin the research process. Indeed, without it there is nothing to animate a research question or design, or to motivate research in the first place. Even strong supporters of research that generates theory will have gone into the field with some preconceived ideas of what they were looking for. As will become apparent, the 'quantitative–qualitative' divide among researchers, who disagree about the role of theory in research and, above all, about 'the sequence and relationship of activities involved' (Robson, 1995, 18) in the process, is rarely reflected in real-life research projects.

Although presenting research methods as free from ontological and epistemological assumptions (see chapter 2 for an explanation of these terms) is not usual, I maintain that this is true until a researcher from a particular discipline employs them. The point here is to show you that your *choice* of methods should not be governed by your discipline but by their appropriateness in answering the questions you have asked. These themes will be revisited in the following chapters.

The structure of the book

The book is divided into five chapters, as shown in figure 1.

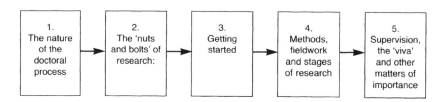

Figure 1 The structure of the book

Chapter 1 introduces the nature of doctoral research. Following the introduction, there is an overview of some of the most important factors making up the doctoral process, including applying to external funding bodies, and the tension apparent in attempting to contribute to knowledge on the one hand, and obtaining a good job and qualification on the other. Two key topics in postgraduate research are discussed: where to study, and time management, both of which are linked to the external parameters set by funding agencies and universities. The final section, 'Before you start', reveals how you can save yourself a lot of time by following some simple advice in the early stages of the research process. After the suggested reading at the end of the chapter, I have included a brief discussion of other books on (postgraduate) research, in order to show how the present book fits in.

An introduction to, and discussion of, the all-important tools and terminology which make up the 'nuts and bolts' of research, and by which research is conducted, is the subject of **chapter 2's** second section. The aim is to demystify the terminology and to reveal the core theoretical and analytical questions that must be addressed in any piece of research. As I have already suggested, it is only with a clear understanding of the terminology employed in research and the underlying issues this terminology reflects that you can begin planning your project. You are advised to reflect not only on the variety of meanings of a specific concept, but on its origins. Chapter 2 also briefly discusses and clarifies key concepts, such as methods (associated with quantitative and qualitative research), methodology, theory, ideal types, typologies and paradigms. Included here is a discussion on the role of theory in research which explores the reasons why theory is needed and how it can assist our enquiries. This section attempts to begin to clarify some of the mystery associated with theoretical application in the social sciences. The idea here, as elsewhere in this book, is not to replace a comprehensive course in research methods, but rather to put you in a position to understand and even enjoy a methods course and to be more reflexive in your own studies. You will also be in a position to identify the essential parts of the research process most relevant to your project.

I then go on to offer some examples of the abuse of certain concepts in the social sciences. The trend of jumping on the 'concept bandwagon' seems to be a familiar one in academia, whereby scholars and students pick up on and employ a concept, taking it out of its original context, simply because it is popular. Finally, a brief section on disciplines, discourses and interdisciplinarity introduces you to some of the differences between, and problems with, academic disciplines and their specificities.

This prepares the way for **chapter 3**, 'Getting started', which turns its attention to the mechanics of research and the beginning of the PhD process. As focusing your topic early is very important, this chapter concentrates on:

- developing research questions and hypotheses with which to guide your research
- the process of defining and refining a research question or hypothesis
- the relationship of the research question or hypothesis to the methods and sources to be employed in the empirical section of your thesis.

The importance of arriving at a set of research questions or hypotheses cannot be overstated, for without specific questions you will not be able to organise your fieldwork. As I have suggested above, this is not to imply that research questions cannot be generated from fieldwork (the inductive method). However, on a pragmatic level, few students have the time or funds to gather sufficient quantities of data with the intention of finding relevant questions or observing specific phenomena, especially as most have to present funding bodies with an outline or plan for fieldwork in the first place.

Chapter 3 introduces the notion of a continuum of literature reviews, ranging from the most common starting point of research (i.e. familiarising yourself with a topic) to speed-reading texts after fieldwork and data analysis. Once you have developed some general research questions or hypotheses, you can start considering what type of fieldwork and level of analysis to undertake.

Chapter 4 opens with a discussion of some examples of methods commonly used to collect and analyse empirical data, including interviews, participant observation, documentary analysis and media analysis. Again, the purpose of the methods section is not to offer a comprehensive account of types of procedures for data collection and analysis, but rather to introduce a series of empirical methods and to indicate how the choice of which ones to use in a study is governed by a certain *logic* contained in the methodology employed or the rationale of the research. The rest of the chapter gives an overview of data collection and fieldwork. These are, to a great extent, the products of choices made about the types of questions asked and the level of analysis and methods chosen with which to answer them.

The chapter then goes on to explore the possible sequencing of research stages, an idea that simplifies and facilitates the research process, and one which external funders of research expect to see. Here I offer a guideline to the process of research that should be adapted and adjusted to suit individual needs and circumstances. As I will show, it is important for students to *imagine* the direction their research will take at a very early stage. Breaking the research process up into manageable and comprehensible stages is all part of a successful research strategy, so long as you retain a sense of the whole project (see Bartov, 1997, 35–50, who disagrees with the idea of research stages). Students will see that there is an inherent logic, albeit not always the same in each case, to the research process and that the stages presented impact greatly on one another and are interlinked.

The final **chapter (5)** discusses some important matters which will impact directly on whether you finish and pass your thesis. The chapter begins by looking at the nature of the supervisor–student relationship and at supervision in general. It is important to consider these factors before beginning your studies, so that you get the most out of them. The failure to complete a doctorate often seems to be due to a student–supervisor mismatch. The second section offers a summary of the viva experience. There is surprisingly little written on this, perhaps one of the most important days of a doctoral candidate's life. This section demystifies the process by drawing on my own experience and that of long-serving professionals and by unpacking the significance, meaning, process and various outcomes of the viva itself. The third section touches on the actual writing of your thesis and some ideas about how to publish your PhD and how to get published in journals. The next section deals with the ethics of research and the issue of plagiarism. Whilst the former has always been important, the latter has become increasingly so, especially as the Internet now offers an unquantifiable amount of easily accessible information to students.

The penultimate section of chapter 5 includes a discussion of how to get the best out of workshops, seminars and conferences and the value of building networks for assisting your studies. The concluding section sums up some of the skills needed to complete a doctorate. As you will see, they are also transferable, employment-related skills that can be applied in a number of settings inside or outside academia.

Appendix 1 includes a glossary of some of the key terms used and often misunderstood in social science research. All of the terms in **bold** in the main text can be found in the glossary. The glossary can be used as a reference guide while reading this and other texts, but will remain a useful companion throughout the course of research. The choice of terms has been driven by their importance for postgraduate research in social science, with a focus on the–building blocks essential to most research.

Finally, **Appendix 2** gives some examples of referencing systems.

1 The nature of doctoral research

Introduction

This book is not a compendium of research methods, methodologies and terminology. Rather, I offer you an introduction to social research in the social sciences. The aim of this first chapter is to begin to familiarise you, as a postgraduate student, with the nature, tools and terminology of the research process. Central to my aims is the 'demystification' of postgraduate research in its various degree structures: MA, MPhil, PhD and DPhil. The emphasis is on *doctoral research*, but many of the terms and much of the process will be applicable to all postgraduate research. The tips and advice will also be of interest to researchers who have to write lengthy dissertations or structured research reports. Much of what follows will be of relevance to research in general, but some specific points about obtaining a higher degree qualification need to be highlighted:

- students must demonstrate a degree of originality in their work
- students must demonstrate that they have successfully completed research training, that is, they need to be in a position to formulate research questions and justify the use of specific research methods.

I intend to take you through the most important aspects of the research process and clarify many of the **concepts** used in social science and the humanities. Two qualifications are needed straight away: first, I do not offer a blueprint for undertaking postgraduate research, but suggest logical stages of research that, once understood, make the prospect of completing a lengthy project less daunting. Second, I approach the process of developing postgraduate research from a *social science* angle, but not from any specific discipline within the social sciences. The building blocks of research are similar for all disciplines with a social science focus. It is the order and level of importance given to the core components of research, and the philosophical assumptions that underlie them, that distinguishes one discipline's methodological approach from another.

The PhD process can be shrouded in mystery. Yet it can be successfully completed by anyone who has a certain amount of intelligence, and, importantly, the degree of commitment necessary. This is not to suggest that obtaining a doctorate is easy. Commitment and steely determination are essential, but of little use if not accompanied by an open and enquiring mind and a willingness to take criticism and advice and to listen and learn from others. Herein lies the first difficulty: to complete a higher degree successfully, you will have to reassess and recalibrate your often deeply held opinions in the light of the new material, arguments and debates you will encounter on your learning journey. It is almost certain that your initial topic, and its underlying assumptions, will differ from your final thesis, as your hunches are checked against evidence and your opinions are shaped and formed by the process of learning.

The nature of the doctoral process

The nature of the doctoral process has changed considerably in recent years in the UK, and this book is informed by a sense of pragmatism that is geared to reflect these changes. According to Robert Cowen, the PhD process has become increasingly bureaucratised – that is, the doctorate is 'less and less a test of original critical intellectual power', but increasingly a 'test of self-organization [and] of institutional organization' (Cowen, 1999, 184). There is no doubt that the doctoral process is now to be understood as an *apprenticeship* in which transferable skills are learnt, skills that can be used within and beyond an academic setting. Emphasis is now placed on the (limited) time period of study, learning the essentials (research methods) and completing specific stages of research (literature review, methods chapters and so on). External bodies, especially the ESRC (Economic and Social Research Council) and increasingly the AHRB (Arts and Humanities Research Board) in the UK, tend to set detailed guidelines for doctoral research, prescribing specific skills and training that institutions must deliver in order to gain their recognition and hence eligibility for receipt of funded students (see below on applying to these institutions). University departments cannot afford to do without external recognition – a kind of quality 'Kitemark' (a sign of excellence) – even if the actual numbers of students supported by these bodies may be small in relation to the aggregate number of doctoral students in the UK. This more structured approach may make the job of obtaining a doctorate more manageable and, providing you have enough time to reflect on your work, it can still be a fulfilling experience as well as useful for your career. Throughout I assume that you will be under demanding financial and time constraints, as most university regulations dictate that doctorates are completed within three or four years, and postgraduate funding is extremely scarce. If a doctoral candidate does not finish within the specified time, the department in which he or she is studying may suffer as a consequence, as continued recognition is closely linked to completion rates.

The first thing to note about a PhD is what it is not. It is rarely a 'magnum opus', the study of all studies ever on a specific topic (many educational systems cater for this by offering a higher doctorate option. This is not usual in the UK). There is plenty of time to produce this afterwards, as most great thinkers in fact did. For example, Albert Einstein and Karl Marx made relatively modest contributions to their fields of research in their doctoral theses, but they spent that time learning the tools of their trade whilst 'demonstrating their fully professional mastery of the established **paradigms**' in their field (Phillips and Pugh, 1994, 35).

Undertaking a PhD should be seen as a learning process, an apprenticeship in the art of research in which you will learn to reflect on the origins of theories and concepts, how to theorise, how to mesh theory with practice, and how to prioritise and organise a vast quantity of material into a readable text within a restricted period of time. The discipline necessary for successfully completing a doctorate will benefit the student far beyond the walls of academia. As already indicated, a capacity for understanding is a useful resource when undertaking doctoral studies, but it is a necessary rather than a sufficient condition. In addition, you will need a mixture of patience, staying power, discipline, interest and intelligence to carry out the task at hand. And, importantly, the willingness to reflect upon and adapt the pre-existing assumptions (sometimes called the 'baggage' we bring with us to the research process) that are the result of all our previous academic and life experiences. This is an important point, because many students – and many academics – stick to a particular way of interpreting evidence, arguments or perspectives through thick and thin and in light of new approaches, simply because something has remained unchallenged for a long time. There is no doubt that a solid formal education will help you undertake a doctorate, but other factors such as mental agility, inquisitiveness, motivation and discipline, which can be acquired outside the school gates, are also beneficial.

Applying to funding bodies

There is no secret formula for successful applications to funding bodies for postgraduate support, but a few general points can be made. The deadline for submission of completed applications is traditionally 1 May, therefore you need to start the application process well in advance of this date, preferably around January. First, you need to decide under which funding body your project falls. Broadly speaking, the ESRC covers social science topics while the AHRB covers more humanities-based projects. There is an area of overlap between the two, and you need to clarify this before sending off your application. The best way to start is by checking the Websites of both bodies (for the ESRC: www.esrc.ac.uk; for the AHRB: www.ahrb.ac.uk), where you can find a joint statement by both funders on the areas they cover. Download *all* the relevant information, including the guidelines on how to fill out the form. Give yourself time to become very familiar with the form, the guidelines on how to fill it in and the exact information and documentation requested. As you will see, much of the documentation (references, confirmation of your degree results and so on) needs to be organised well in advance of the deadline. You should set about drawing up a provisional timetable of things to do. If you already have a place where you are going to study, you will be able to draw on the institution's and its staff's expertise in putting the forms together. Quite apart from the fact that you will need to produce an outstanding application to qualify for an award, you also need to attend to the very detailed application form, ensuring you give the funding bodies all the information they need. In general, the ESRC form is the harder to complete and will therefore need more time. A great deal more work will have to be given over to the actual proposal than for the AHRB form, which requires far fewer details than the ESRC's. The content of your proposal and its structure will therefore depend on which grant you apply for. It is likely that in the future the AHRB will require a more detailed proposal of a doctoral project.

The ESRC no longer funds stand-alone MAs, thus the shift in emphasis to funding four-year doctorates will probably result in even fiercer competition among students for the coveted awards. In this case, the need to produce precise and clear proposals is even more important. The thing that divides equally qualified applicants (I think a *very* good upper-second or first-class degree is almost a prerequisite to qualify for an award) is the ability to communicate the following (see chapter 2 for clarification of the terms used):

- a crisp and clear summary of the problem to be tackled
- an indication of how the proposed project fits in with the wider, relevant literature
- a discussion of the theoretical approach adopted
- a number of clearly set-out research questions or hypotheses
- a discussion of the methods to be employed to answer, refute or validate research questions or hypotheses
- an awareness of relevant data sources and data analysis
- a timetable for the completion of the thesis.

It takes a lot of drafting and redrafting to cram all this information into the space allowed on the form, so begin the process as soon as possible (for help on how to come up with ideas and research questions, see chapter 3).

Remember, too, that many departments offer scholarships, bursaries, fee-waivers or GTAs (Graduate Teaching Assistantships) as alternative ways of supporting your studies. Many postgraduates manage to teach while they are studying, although there is a balance to be struck. Teaching will help you to gain invaluable experience and earn some extra money, but it must not distract from the job at hand: finishing your studies. Realistically, for a full-time doctoral student, 3–4 hours a week teaching is the maximum, given that you need to prepare for class, mark students' work and probably travel to and from your place of work.

Between contributing to knowledge and gaining qualifications

This book is designed not *just* to assist you in obtaining a doctorate within three years, but *also* to help you make a worthwhile contribution to existing debates by providing the tools and the confidence to achieve this. Fear of the unknown, the esoteric and the complex only hinders progress. By seeing the research process stripped bare, revealing the factors that constitute good scholarship, you will be in a position to overcome these fears. I assume that anyone reading this text will have, or will be finishing, a first or second degree (most institutions insist on at least an upper-second-class degree as a prerequisite to undertaking doctoral research or even a Master's; there are exceptions, however, and mature students, in particular, may be able to provide evidence of different, but equivalent levels of attainment). The distance between a solid MA (Master of Arts; *Magister Artium*) dissertation and a PhD is less great than that between BA

(Bachelor of Arts; *Baccalaureus Artium*) and PhD (Doctor of Philosophy; *Philosophea Doctor*), as the Master's student will already have had to contend with many issues confronting a doctoral candidate. The leap from a BA to a PhD is great, but not unbridgeable. The most obvious unique aspect of doctoral research is the emphasis it places on the individual. There are few taught elements of the degree, except for research training, and the student is expected to have a high level of self-discipline in order to be able to cope with only minimal guidance and structure – in comparison to what students at BA or MA level are used to. Self-discipline, of course, is easier to produce if you have a keen interest in a subject, or if the reason for starting on the road to a higher degree is clear.

Why are you undertaking postgraduate research in the first place? It may be to simply progress up the career ladder, or to obtain a certain type of job; I hope, perhaps, a combination of both of these, with a desire to undertake a piece of original research (essential for a PhD). Denis Lawton makes a valid point in stating that just because you are interested in something does not necessarily mean you should write a PhD on it. You may be better off producing another kind of book, one without the constraints and 'hoops' a PhD candidate is required to jump through (Lawton, 1999, 3). However, the combination of both your interest and ability should ensure that you have a good chance of being successful over the sustained period of study. The point here is not to do a doctorate for the sake of it. The title 'Dr' may be elevating – for a short while – but that is not a good enough reason for spending at least three years studying hard. As a researcher, you should be aiming to contribute something new to an existing body of knowledge and, if you cannot, you do not have a PhD thesis.

What you should avoid in all cases is to end up simply adding to the increasing mountain of monographs, a scenario in which, as George Steiner puts it: 'the true source of Z's tome is X's and Y's work on the identical subject' (Steiner, 1991, 39). Instead, what you should aim to do is to come as close as possible to what Steiner terms 'the immediate', or, in the manner I interpret it here, the event you are attempting to shed light on or explain. The point of research should not be to give an analysis of a critique of an event, but to deliver an interpretation of the event itself. You need the tertiary material (texts on texts) and the secondary material (others' work on the event) to position and guide your work and to situate your contribution, but the aim is to complement this with primary or new material, or with a novel interpretation. There is a certain tension here with the need to produce original work within a restricted period of time. As I have already suggested, however, time is no guarantee of good scholarship, for if you fail to grasp the fundamentals of the trade, no length of time spent on a research project will produce precise and useful research.

The right place to study

Choosing the right department for you and your project in the first instance is crucial. If there are only two other postgraduates in a given department, one working on a Marxist interpretation of Franz Kafka's *Das Schloss* and the other on an econometric analysis of the Dollar–Deutschmark exchange rate dynamics, you are not going into the best environment for, say, studying the role of Polish farmers in European integration. Apart from the fact that this department will probably not have a Polish, or perhaps even a European, expert, you will be isolated in your studies with little chance of the type of feedback you require and opportunities to present ongoing work in postgraduate seminars. So, to avoid isolation, choose an institution with a number of postgraduate students and one which offers outlets and forums for discussion. This choice, will, of course, be linked to whether or not you can obtain funding. A good idea is to speak to existing students and ask them about the facilities and opportunities available and, of course, their own research experiences. Don't be frightened to ask about the provision of research methods courses or any specific course you may need for your studies. Ask also about review procedures for monitoring progress, and whether the department has a designated member of staff as postgraduate co-ordinator. These mechanisms should be seen as beneficial to your studies (e.g. supervision meetings, yearly progress panel, student–staff liaison committees and so on), and as ways of adding structure to an otherwise lonely process. This is a far cry from the original ideal of doctoral research developed in Germany by Wilhelm von Humboldt, which was based on *Einsamkeit* (isolation) and *Freiheit* (freedom), both of which are not necessarily virtues, given the conditions and constraints which modern doctoral students face (see Cowen, 1999, 185).

There is a point, of course, at which too many bureaucratic hurdles stifle creative thinking, but too few formalised procedures can lead to isolation and even 'throwing in the towel'. Do not let your choice of department be guided solely by the presence of a renowned scholar – if there are half a dozen in the department then that is fine. Otherwise, leading scholars have a tendency to be in great demand and will almost certainly have a large number of doctoral students, a heavy conference schedule (i.e. they are very often abroad when you need to see them) and may be hard to make an appointment with. Their turnaround time on giving feedback on versions of your work – an important part of your development – could be months. If, however, there are a number of capable scholars in a given department this will be less of a concern, as you will always have somebody with whom you can discuss your ideas, providing your topic chimes with the research interests of the department. Remember, too, the dangers associated with all supervisors, celebrities or not; these include:

- you doing your supervisor's project
- you never being able to come up with an original idea (because he or she has been there, done that, etc.)
- a general lack of confidence in your own judgements and an over-reliance on the supervisor and, especially, his or her knowledge of the subject.

You do need, however, someone who knows what an MPhil or PhD consists of, and who is at least halfway *interested* in your subject area and is sensitive to how *you* want to approach it. Ideally, you should seek joint supervision, something discussed in more detail in chapter 5.

Matters of time

Good time-management skills are of paramount importance in research, and now is the moment to give these some thought. A slow start will inevitably translate into a mad rush towards the end of the period of study. The freedom afforded by full-time doctoral studies – that is, if you do not have to work at the same time – can lead to bad time management. Try not to get into the habit of burning the midnight oil and waking up at two o'clock in the afternoon. A good night's sleep and a regular work pattern will probably lead to better results in the end. Remember also to leave time for life outside PhD research, as merely immersing yourself in your studies without coming up for air could lead to a number of problems. First, you need time off from direct studying, so that you can recover, absorb and reflect on everything you have been thinking, reading and writing about. Second, if you give up previous hobbies or socialising to fit in a few extra hours' reading, the results may be counter-productive. You need to feel 'balanced' within yourself, a state that will obviously differ from person to person (see May, 1999, 62–3). This is, after all, what you will hopefully aspire to post-PhD, so you may as well start now.

Reasons for bad time management are manifold: for example, the perfectionist who refuses to write but continues to gather data will eventually be buried under a pile of information with little or nothing to show for it. The perfectionist would also not have had the benefit of frequent exchanges with his or her supervisor and thus run the risk of 'going off at a tangent', that is, digressing from their area of enquiry. Perfectionism may be a virtue to some, but under conditions of tight time constraints, it could prevent a person from actually achieving anything. Other reasons for delays include distraction from the task at hand. This can come in many forms, including having to work to make ends meet – a particular concern for many part-time students holding down a job. Once the research momentum is broken, it is very difficult to find your way back in. Therefore postgraduate studies demand constant application and concentration for a particular period of time, and students ought to ask themselves whether they are willing to enter into this commitment before beginning their studies. On the positive side, research is a gradual process of accumulating knowledge, which brings with it a sense of achievement and confidence, that in turn makes the whole process more enjoyable and may lead to publication or conference papers en route.

Your choice of subject

A clear idea of what you want to study (once you have sorted out the question of why) will assist in getting you off to a good start. Begin by drawing up a shortlist of areas of interest, bearing in mind that these have to correspond with the interests of your chosen department, or at least someone in it. Narrow your topic area as soon as you can. This is not to suggest that the 'what' – or starting point – of research is static, for this may shift and be redefined in the light of subsequent work, but *it is essential to narrow your focus at an early stage on a specific area*. For example, you may begin by saying 'I'm interested in French foreign policy'. This is obviously a potentially vast area, covering security issues, inter-state relations and the expression of one state's interests vis-à-vis others, etc. At an early stage, you need to draw on previous experience, 'gut' feelings or hunches and personal interest to narrow the focus of your research to a specific area, say bilateral relations between France and the UK. By narrowing the focus, you can begin to dip into the literature on Franco-British bilateral relations, scanning texts to see what has and, importantly, what has not, been written on the subject. We will return to a similar example when discussing the mechanics of research.

Before you start

There are a number of things that will make the research process far more productive and enjoyable and allow you to 'hit the ground running'. This section touches on things that ought to be done *before* you start your research project. These range from learning to assess the manageability of your project, to getting to know what it is that constitutes an MA, MPhil or PhD in the first place. Taking some time at the beginning of your studies to familiarise yourself with what lies before you will save time in the long run: often it is the 'hares' who throw themselves into writing their dissertations or theses with little consideration for university regulations, thesis format or word length, who are overtaken by the 'tortoises' who allowed themselves sufficient time to study the research terrain before beginning.

Surprisingly, many postgraduate students do not have a clue what their **dissertation** or **thesis** is supposed to consist of beyond the word-limit and, perhaps, the intimidatory sentence in university handbooks (for PhDs) calling for 'works that contribute substantially to human knowledge'. This sentence is enough to put off the brightest student. The point here is, if you do not know what constitutes the degree you are aiming for, you are not going to be able to map out a plan of how to get there. Imagine training for a race and not knowing the distance to be run. It is no good being a good sprinter if the race turns out to be over 10 miles. Hence, you will need to familiarise yourself with what is expected of you *before* you begin. By looking at past theses of previous students from your department – they are usually all collected in the main university library – you can learn several things. What is the average length? What is the ratio of empirical material to the literature review and theoretical approach in your particular department and topic area? Familiarise yourself with the structure of the theses and, after a while, a pattern may emerge. Here is a standard example, which will assist in highlighting specific components of research (however, bear in mind that this is only one model of research and it should *not be considered as fixed*):

• introduction
• literature review
• methodology
• case study(ies)/empirical section
• evaluation
• conclusion.

This example is certainly valid for many standard social science theses. In the humanities, however, the stages highlighted above may be less pronounced. You will, however, have a beginning and an end. You must also connect your thesis with a wider literature (number 2. above) and your thesis will exhibit, perhaps implicitly, a methodology and a case study or subject. You will also have to evaluate and sum up your work. The difference is that in the social sciences, the above sections are more likely to be clearly distinguishable from one another. The simple advice here is that you should acquaint yourself with the task ahead. By having a rough idea of what you are aiming at, you manage to dispel many myths and anxieties and you can already begin to have a mental picture of the logic of research. By breaking down the thesis into broad parts, as in the example above, you can begin to get a feel of what it comprises.

Subsequent chapters will deal with these stages of research in more detail, clarifying the relationship between the constituent parts. Once you have familiarised yourself with PhD theses in your department and university, the best advice is to consider the format and presentation of your own work in this light. Usually, the university library will have a pamphlet on how to present a thesis, including page set-up (size of margins), font size, how to use footnotes and references and word-length (check whether this includes or excludes appendices, tables, diagrams, bibliography and footnotes). Look at this before you start any writing, for if you set up your thesis and your computer in the format and style (point size, paragraph, page set-up, etc.) stipulated in your department's or university's regulations, you can use this for all subsequent work on the thesis and you will save yourself no end of trouble when you come to put together the constituent parts of your project. Setting out the format early does not, however, mean that the first sections or ideas you put down on paper are fixed. On the contrary, you will need to go over and re-draft sections and chapters several times before they are actually finished (see chapter 5 for advice on writing your thesis).

Referencing and other tips

It is a very good idea to start proper referencing and a bibliography from the outset, and to decide on the type of referencing system you wish to use (Harvard or Humanities) and stick with it throughout the text. Proper referencing includes noting down accurate records of page numbers, the book, journal or newspaper title, the author and, most easily overlooked and forgotten, the publisher and place and date of publication of the source you are citing from (see appendix 2 for examples of referencing). If you are photocopying from a book or journal, you should also photocopy the title page and the imprints page – the one with all the crucial details on it, usually on the reverse of the title page. When you are photocopying a chapter or article from a book or journal – bearing in mind, of course, the relevant copyright laws – start at the end of the chapter/article and work backwards, so that you end up with the chapter/article in the correct order, thereby saving yourself half an hour of sorting out the page order. Taking care in recording accurate notes will save you an inordinate amount of time (in the time some people spend on searching for lost citations and references they could have written another article). Good and careful note-taking is linked to the notion of academic honesty and the avoidance of plagiarism (Rosamond, 2001). The latter is looked upon as the crime of all crimes in academia and for that reason warrants its own section in chapter 5. I therefore reiterate the need to get into the habit of comprehensively recording bibliographical details of all the reading you undertake, as you will forget the precise reference quite quickly, which may become a problem if you, or someone else, discovers at a later date that an apparently unrelated article is actually germane to your thesis.

Whatever referencing system you use, you must be careful not to mix practices together, by using endnotes, footnotes and references in the main text. You can, however, use both references and footnotes, with the latter providing additional information other than on the sources used. Your choice of referencing system, again, may be governed by your department's regulations, so it is best to check, as wasted hours can be spent reformatting footnotes to endnotes and vice versa. Many a student – and senior academic too – has spent several weeks at the end of their studies scrambling around redoing footnotes or endnotes that were left behind unfinished in a creative burst of intellectual activity somewhere in year one. Another factor to consider is the referencing system used by the academic journals that you aspire to publish in. The Harvard system, used in this book, is one of the easiest and most popular, because it is quick, efficient, and does not require a great number of footnotes. Remember from day one to keep an accurate note of all the books and articles you have read or cited in a bibliographical list. As soon as you find something new, get into the habit of adding it to the list immediately. Remember, also, if you are using foreign texts in your analysis, to look up the regulations on translations *before* you start, as this will have profound implications on the length of your thesis and the time you may have to spend on translating into English.

Familiarise yourself with the 'hardware' of research, that is, all of the resources you are likely to need at the institution in which you undertake your research. For example, the library: what has it got to offer? What about IT courses? Do you have access to a computer? You need to be able to master the computer, use e-mail and the Internet (on-line searching of material using databases and specific Web sites for research in the social sciences and humanities is rapidly increasing) and, if you plan to undertake quantitative analysis, a package such as SPSS (Statistical Package in the Social Sciences).

A mistake that almost all postgraduates and academics will make at one point in their studies concerns saving data on floppy disks and on the hard drive of their computers. As you will be writing something in the region of three hundred pages and more for your thesis and notes, there is every reason to take great care when storing such information. First, make sure, if you are using computers at the university and one at home, that all computers have compatible word-processing programs. Use Rich Text Format (RTF) as far as possible, as this can be read and understood by most computer software. There is nothing more frustrating than saving work in one format only to find out once you arrive home or at work that your computer is unable to decipher the rows of hieroglyphics. Second, make sure you back up your work on disks, so that even if your computer(s) explodes or is stolen, you still have a faithful copy of your manuscript to hand. Also, set your computer, or have it set, to save your work every few minutes in case of a crash or power cut. The third point relates to the discussion above on referencing: record and log *all* your footnotes and bibliographical references *as you proceed*. If you manage to get into this habit, it will save you hours and spare your nerves in the latter stages of your project. Finally, make sure you have an up-to-date virus detector on your computer(s), as a single virus could destroy hours of work in one click of the mouse.

Professional associations

At the beginning of your studies, you should consider joining an association relevant to your thesis topic, for example, the PSA (Political Studies Association) or the BSA (British Sociological Association). Each discipline will have a specific association through which you gain access to a number of useful things. For example, on joining, usually at a subsidised rate, you can go to annual conferences, workshops and specialist sub-groups that may be more relevant to your topic. Some associations even send out newsletters and journals, both of which are important while you are studying: the newsletter contains information on forthcoming events, and the journal is essential reading for doctoral students working at the 'cutting edge' of research. Look out for e-mail circulation lists that are usually free to join and provide instant updates on conferences, new publications, and so on. Many associations also offer guidance on how to undertake research in specific disciplines. These types of gatherings offer an ideal opportunity for 'networking' among like-minded people, both students and staff: something to bear in mind if you intend staying in academia. In addition, there is something quite reassuring in seeing the face behind the name of an author of a book you have read. You can see that these authors are human after all! Some associations have graduate networks through which you can make contact with people who are working in a similar field or who are experiencing similar problems. A good idea is to have business cards made up at an early stage, as this not only looks more professional but is also more practical than writing e-mail addresses on the back of a napkin. Interaction and a constant exchange of ideas is a good way to prevent isolation, increase your knowledge and enhance your ability to formulate succinctly your own views. This theme is taken up in more detail in chapter 5, when I discuss the use you can make of workshops, conferences, etc. Equally, make use of open or graduate seminars in your department and beyond, even if the topic is not directly linked to your own, in order to observe how others present their work, define concepts and develop **hypotheses.** This will, directly or indirectly, impact on and inform the way in which you choose to define your own concepts and develop your own hypotheses.

If this chapter has not gone far enough in demystifying the popular conception that doctoral research requires the brain capacity of a Hegel, then the explanation of research terms and the breakdown of logical research steps in the following chapters, I hope, will.

Summary

The first chapter has introduced the purpose of this book, which can be summed up as demystifying the postgraduate research process. As I have pointed out, many of the terms, stages and problems encountered in this process will be relevant to doctorates and other postgraduate research degrees. Central to this book is actually *doing* a doctorate, and for this reason, this chapter has highlighted the following:

- The nature of doctoral studies and especially the tension between time pressure, gaining qualifications and producing good scholarship
- The need to reflect on why you are undertaking a doctorate in the first place
- The need to consider carefully, as far as it is possible given financial constraints, the place where you choose to study
- You need a regular working pattern to achieve the best results
- You should find out exactly what it is you are supposed to do in order to obtain the degree you are studying for
- You should familiarise yourself as soon as possible with your institution's referencing system and start a bibliography from day one
- You should consider joining a professional association linked to your area of interest

Further reading

Burnham, P. (ed.) (1997) *Surviving the Research Process in Politics,* London/Washington, Pinter.

Graves, N and Varma, V. (eds.) (1999) *Working for a Doctorate. A Guide for the Humanities and Social Sciences:* London/New York, Routledge, especially chapters 1, 4 and 10.

Phillips, E. M. and Pugh, D. S. (eds.) (1994) *How to Get a PhD: A Handbook for Students and Their Supervisors,* Buckingham/Philadelphia: Open University Press.

Addendum: books on research and doctoral studies

Books abound on the topic of undertaking research, dealing with a variety of factors relevant to the entirety of a research project. The following chapters of this book are more concerned with revealing the logic of research, with an emphasis on demystifying the PhD by unpacking its constituent parts and by shedding light on their relationship to one another. The majority of textbooks on the market deal with the process of research in general. There are a number of good texts that aim to cover a wide range of research situations and levels, relevant to doctoral students as much to seasoned academics, policy makers and practitioners (for example, Bell, 1993; Blaxter *et al.*, 1997; Blaikie, 2000; Robson, 1995). Although these books are not explicitly aimed at Master's or doctoral students, it is to them and their ilk that most postgraduates turn. None of the books available on doctoral research sets out to explain the meaning of key terms and phrases in research. The present book does, however, whilst narrowing its focus specifically on postgraduate research in the social sciences and those parts of humanities which lean towards social science. This allows a more specific and in-depth exposition of the *actual* research process. The following brief overview of the literature focuses on the most well-known books that *explicitly* refer to postgraduate studies.

A recent attempt to focus a particular text on this area was undertaken by Peter Burnham in his edited volume *Surviving the Research Process in Politics* (1997). The result is a multi-authored book consisting of a number of important topics relating to doctoral research. Some chapters have direct relevance to parts of the doctoral process (in politics), while others are more concerned with factors that can influence it, for example, working full-time whilst studying. The book is not designed to explain the building blocks of research or to touch on the inherent logic of the process, but Burnham's useful introductory chapter, and his chapter on the **viva**, along with a few chapters on methods used in research, do shed light on some important components of a PhD. The present book aims to complement such books by giving a blow-by-blow account of the doctoral process, from finding a topic to getting through the viva examination.

Working for a Doctorate (Graves and Varma, 1999) is another useful multi-authored book, with topics ranging from 'Intercultural Issues', and 'Gender Issues' to 'Financing a Doctorate'. Denis Lawton offers an excellent overview of how to succeed in postgraduate studies and Derek May tackles the central issue of time management. The present book brings the core issues relevant to the actual 'nuts and bolts' of PhD research together. This is not to suggest that issues of gender power relations, any form of prejudice, etc., are not extremely important, as these issues are central to the wider parameters in which your doctorate will be researched. However, unlike the present book, *Working for a Doctorate* is not, in the strictest sense, about actually *doing* a PhD.

Perhaps the best known and most widely sold book on PhD research is *How to Get a PhD* (Phillips and Pugh, 1994). This text addresses both the supervisor and the supervisee by offering advice on many aspects of the doctoral process. This necessarily covers a lot of ground, as the book does not narrow its focus to any specific area (e.g. social sciences) which results in a broad **approach** to the PhD project. The Phillips and Pugh book has some very important chapters such as those on psychological aspects of the PhD research and the student–supervisor relationship. Elements of the former (isolation, boredom, frustration, etc.) will not figure greatly here, as the emphasis is to strip bare the mechanics of research and to grasp the terms and terminology associated with it. The student–supervisor relationship will be covered, but solely from the *student's* perspective. None the less, this book, although targeted directly at students, will also be of use to supervisors advising postgraduate students on how to undertake a PhD. It tells students about *actually doing* a doctorate. It sets out the building blocks of postgraduate research by explaining the *terms and terminology* and highlighting the internal *logic* of research. It provides potential doctoral students with a map and a set of signposts through the maze of the research process. Finally, the following chapters have been written in plain and direct English, addressed directly to students themselves.

2 The 'nuts and bolts' of research

Introduction

This chapter continues with the 'demystification' of the postgraduate research process. The first, and most substantial, section deals with the all-important tools and terminology of the research process. With little or no knowledge of the standard reference points in general research, students are likely to produce a piece a work which is unclear and imprecise: learning the rules of the game simplifies the process, makes it transparent and takes away the fear associated with the unknown. This chapter opens with an explanation of the apparently complex terminology of 'onto-logical' and 'epistemological' issues underpinning all forms of research, before introducing the key concepts employed in the social sciences and the humanities, which form the essential components of the research process. Next, I introduce the concepts of methods and methodology, in which the discussion revolves around the quantitative–qualitative distinction in research and the meaning of the term 'methodology'. As will become apparent, methods are central to academic research. This chapter seeks to explain their *purpose* in research, but is not intended to be a substitute for a methods textbook. A selection of the most common research methods used to gather empirical data, from the vast range available, will be introduced in chapter 3.

The next section introduces and discusses some of the bewildering range of analytical devices available to you. These include, starting with the most abstract, theory, and its role, conceptual frameworks, models, ideal types, typologies, paradigms and concepts. There are, of course, many more such devices, but they will all relate to the continuum of analytical tools outlined in this chapter. The penultimate section first takes a look at concepts, the least complex but most widely used tool in research, and then discusses how they are sometimes abused – a habit you would do well to avoid. Finally, there is a section on academic disciplines – which are all predicated on certain assumptions and ideas, themselves much disputed – and the notion of interdisciplinarity and post-disciplinarity.

The tools and terminology of research

As my chief aim is to demystify the research process, there is no better place to start than with the tools and terminology used in academic projects and theses. The following is not intended to be an exhaustive list of research terminology, but rather an introduction to some of the key components used in developing a research proposal and those most relevant to undertaking postgraduate research.

Why do we need to know and understand standard terms and concepts in social science? A simple example will suffice: consider a would-be bricklayer who does not know the difference between a trowel, a spirit level and a chisel. These are the basic tools of his trade, without which no wall can be built. Each tool has a specific purpose and, if he misuses them, for example, trying to lay bricks with a chisel, the results will be disastrous. In research, specific tools have specific purposes and, if we are to use them correctly, we must first understand what they mean, what they are meant to do and how and when to use them. A good starting point in learning about the tools and terminology of research is to look at the most commonly misunderstood terms, **ontology** and **epistemology**.

Ontology

Ontology is the image of social reality upon which a theory is based – i.e. the 'claims and assumptions that are made about the nature of social reality, claims about what exists, what it looks like, what units make it up and how these units interact with each other. In short, ontological assumptions are concerned with what we believe constitutes social reality' (Blaikie, 2000, 8). With this in mind, it is not difficult to understand how different scholarly traditions embedded in fundamentally different cultural contexts can have diverging views of the world and differing assumptions underpinning their particular approaches to social enquiry. An individual's ontological position is their 'answer to the question: what is the nature of the social and political reality to be investigated?' (Hay, 2002, 3), an assumption which is difficult, if not impossible, to refute empirically (ibid., 4). Examples of ontological positions are those contained within the approaches known as 'objectivism' and 'constructivism'. Broadly speaking, the former is 'an ontological position that asserts that social phenomena and their meanings have an existence that is independent of social actors'. The latter, on the other hand, is an alternative ontological position that 'asserts that social phenomena and their meanings are continually being accomplished by social actors. It implies that social phenomena and categories are not only produced through social interaction but that they are in a constant state of revision' (Bryman, 2001, 16-18). It is clear from these two examples how one's ontological position will affect the manner in which one undertakes research.

If ontology is about what we may know, then epistemology is about how we come to know what we know.

Epistemology

Epistemology, one of the core branches of philosophy, is concerned with the theory of knowledge, especially with regard to its methods, validation and 'the possible ways of gaining knowledge of social reality, whatever it is understood to be. In short, claims about how what is assumed to exist can be known' (ibid.). Derived from the Greek words *episteme* (knowledge) and *logos* (reason), epistemology focuses on the knowledge-gathering process and is concerned with developing new models or theories that are better than competing models and theories. Knowledge, and the ways of discovering it, are not static, but forever changing. When reflecting on theories, and concepts in general, you need to think about the assumptions on which they are based and where they originate from. For example, do they stem from America or Europe (this will have an impact on the overall outcome of the research and its generalisability, otherwise known as external validity, or universal laws)? Can theories generated in western democracies properly explain phenomena in east European transition states with a 60-year history of authoritarianism? Two contrasting epistemological positions are those contained within the approaches known as 'positivism' and 'interpretivism'. Broadly speaking, the former is 'an epistemological position that advocates the application of the methods of the natural sciences to the study of social reality and beyond'. The latter, on the other hand, can be seen as an epistemological position that is 'predicated upon the view that a strategy is required that respects the differences between people and the objects of the natural sciences and therefore requires the social scientist to grasp the subjective meaning of social action' (Bryman, 2001,

12–13. See Bryman's chapter 1 for a thorough discussion of ontological and epistemological issues). It is clear that choosing one of these epistemological positions will lead you to employ a *different* methodology than you would were you to choose the other. It is also clear to see how a researcher's ontological and epistemological positions can lead to different views of the same social phenomena.

Differing ontological and epistemological views

The assumptions underlying theories are thus both epistemological and ontological. Plato's famous allegory of the cave is strikingly instructive in making us aware of the root of ontology and epistemology, for it shows how very different perceptions of what constitutes reality can exist. Prisoners in a cave are chained in such a way that they can only look directly in front of them, at a wall upon which shadows of artefacts, carried by people behind the prisoners, are cast by the light of a fire. The prisoners give names and characteristics to these objects, which, to them, represent reality. Plato then imagines a scene in which one prisoner leaves the dark cave and sees that not only are the shapes on the wall shadows of objects, but also that the objects themselves are effigies of reality. In the text, Socrates, in conversation with Glaucon, says:

> Suppose someone tells him [the prisoner released from the cave] that what he's been seeing all this time has no substance, and that he's now closer to reality and is seeing more accurately, because of the greater reality of the things in front of his eyes – what do you imagine his reaction would be? And what do you think he'd say if he were shown any of the passing objects and had to respond to being asked what it was? Don't you think he'd be bewildered and would think that there was more reality in what he'd been seeing before than in what he was being shown now? (Plato, 1994, 241–2)

This passage mirrors how some people can come to think in certain ways, which are bound by certain cultural and social norms and parameters, for example, those established by academic disciplines. Any premises built upon the experience of the cave dwellers are certain to differ from those put forward by men and women who live outside the cave. It is for this reason that we need to be aware, and understand, that *different* views of the world and *different* ways of gathering knowledge exist. Finally, the order in which I have discussed the two terms in this section is important, for 'ontology logically precedes epistemology which logically precedes methodology' (i.e. how we go about acquiring the knowledge which exists. See below for an explanation of methodology; Hay, 2002, 5).

In your time as a postgraduate student, you will undoubtedly come across the perennial conference hack who insists on asking speakers at seminars and conferences about their ontological or epistemological standpoints, possibly with the hope of concealing the fact that they know little about the actual subject matter being presented. To guard against this, but much more importantly, to appreciate the deep importance of the foundations of approaches to research, you need to become familiar with the terminology through which we understand the research process. Familiarity with academic terms is part of research: the earlier you gain it, the better your chances of success and enjoyment – and the less chance of getting caught out by our conference hack. The remainder of this chapter will take you through some of the concepts central to postgraduate studies and research in general.

Key concepts in research

Methods

At the root of all research lies what the ancient Greeks termed *methodos*. On the one hand, the term means 'the path towards knowledge' and on the other, 'reflections on the quest for knowledge-gathering'. Many of the central concerns of research have their roots firmly in the work of ancient Greek philosophers. Witness, for example, the manner in which Socrates, Plato and Aristotle employed classificatory systems or typologies of states, types of rule, etc., to make sense of the social phenomena surrounding them.

I follow Norman Blaikie's (2000) more modern definition of **methods** and **methodology**, two words that are often confused, used interchangeably and generally misunderstood (see also Blaxter *et al.*, 1997, 59). The former is easier to explain and understand than the latter. Research methods, quite simply, can be seen as the 'techniques or procedures used to collate and analyse data' (Blaikie, 2000, 8). The method(s) chosen for a research project are inextricably linked to the **research questions** posed and to the **sources** of data collected. For example, if I wish to understand how the policy on a specific issue was made in the European Commission, I would have to think of a way of obtaining information with which to answer this question. One method could be to speak to those who implement policy, or, probably better still, those people who work for key decision-makers in the Commission. In interviews (either structured, semi-structured or unstructured – see chapter 4) with key people, I would have to pose questions in such a way as to shed light on the specific area of policy-making in which I was interested. The interviewees may, if I am lucky, point me to specific documents or further discussion partners. Thus, my original question has led me to:

- the interview technique
- interview transcripts
- (possibly) key documents as source material to analyse.

Research methods come in all shapes and sizes, ranging from in-depth interviews, statistical inference, discourse analysis and archival research of historical documents to participant observation (see chapter 4 for a brief overview of the most common types of method). The choice of methods will be influenced by ontological and epistemological assumptions and, of course, the questions you are asking, and the *type* of project you are undertaking, e.g. either researching individuals' attitudes or institutional change. However, methods themselves should be seen as *free from ontological and epistemological assumptions*, and the choice of which to use should be guided by your research questions. In the minds of many researchers, certain methods are inextricably bound up with certain ontological and epistemological assumptions: for example, try asking an enthusiastic rational-choice theorist what he or she thinks of discourse analysis. The important thing to note here is that it is the researcher who employs a par- ticular method in a particular way, thereby associating it with a specific set of ontological assumptions. It is not the method that approaches scholarship with pre-existing baggage, but rather the researcher. However, within the academic community, some methods are looked upon and associated with 'good social science', whilst others are not. Remember that good scholarship is not just the result of a specific method, but the result of *how* you employ, cross-check, collate and analyse the data that methods assist you in collecting. Your work should be judged on how its constituent parts logically link together, not by which methods you use.

A doctorate without any method, however loosely defined, is an out- and-out contradiction. In research, methods have two principal functions:

- they offer the researcher a way of gathering information or gaining insight into a particular issue
- they enable another researcher to re-enact the first's endeavours by emulating the methods employed.

The former is essential for concentrating and narrowing our line of enquiry when analysing a particular topic. The latter is essential in **validating** research. The centrality of methods in postgraduate research is borne out by the frequency with which the question 'Why have you chosen this method as opposed to another?' is posed in the viva (see chapter 5).

Methods can be used in either **quantitative research**, which is concerned predominantly with quantity, or **qualitative research**, which is concerned with interpreting the subjective experiences, i.e. the perspectives, of the individuals being studied. Although these research approaches are different, the logic of **inference** underlying both types of enquiry may be the same, rendering the sharp distinction between them that is often made a false one (Landman, 2000, 19; Silverman, 2000, 11). Equally, both qualitative and quantitative research must be understood as umbrella terms, under which a wide and diverse range of 'paradigms, approaches to data, and methods for the analysis of data' are categorised (Punch, 2000a, 139).

Quantitative research
Broadly speaking, quantitative research is characterised by three basic phases: finding **variables** for concepts, **operationalising** them in the study, and measuring them. This type of research **approach** tends, in general, to 'abstract from particular instances to seek general description or to test causal hypotheses; it seeks measurements and analyses that are easily replicable by other researchers' (King *et al.*, 1994, 3). (Of course, not all quantification satisfies King's statement, the use of quantitative methods in discourse analysis being a case in point). The replication of methods is seen by supporters of quantitative analyses as very important, because the work is thus subject to **verifiability**, which provides an air of legitimacy, reproducibility, reliability and objectivity. Statistical reliability is sought by undertaking a random sample of cases (the more the better) from which generalisable results can be gleaned. Therefore, studies employing quantitative methods are more often than not carried out involving a number of cases or subjects, which are independent of context, or, to put it another way, they are studies in which the researcher does not physically interact with the subject of analysis. A case in point would be an analysis based on statistics of several countries' welfare states. These statistics can be collated from various sources, without having to visit the countries involved. In this type of research, the researcher is said to be detached from the object of study (Neuman, 2000, 16). Of course, no one can be fully detached from any type of research – or offer a **value-free** analysis – precisely because researchers are the sum of their

accumulated knowledge, which will be based on certain assumptions about the world.

Quantitative research, pejoratively known as 'number-crunching', uses techniques that apply more to numerical data. Researchers develop variables or concepts which can be measured, and convert them into specific data-collection techniques. These techniques produce precise numerical information which can be understood as the empirical representation of the (abstract) concepts (Neuman, 2000, 157–8). Quantitative techniques include identifying general patterns and relationships among variables, testing hypotheses and theories and making predictions based on these results (Ragin 1994, 132–6). Some statistical packages and models require a fairly high level of mathematical knowledge, whilst other packages, for example SPSS (Statistical Package in the Social Sciences), do a lot of the calculations for you. The researcher must, however, be in a position to *interpret* the statistics the program produces. When using statistics, they also need to be aware of sampling error and the potential biases in any interpretation of findings. The most common types of method associated with quantitative research are social surveys, analyses of previously collected data or official statistics and 'structured' observation (Silverman, 2000, 3; this method is discussed in chapter 4). Quantitative researchers may seek correlations between variables, but they are often 'reluctant to move from statements of **correlation** to **causal** statements' (ibid., 4), as the complexity of social life makes it difficult to be absolutely certain that a particular variable is the sole cause of something. While a firm understanding of the role statistics play in our lives and in much scholarship is essential, whether you intend to employ them in your study or not, you need to be aware that some facets of human action, especially behavioural phenomena, are difficult to capture or 'measure' quantitatively. Many critics of quantitative research are quick to pick up on this, suggesting that 'there are areas of social reality which such statistics cannot measure' (Silverman, 2000, 8); an example here would be the concept of trust (see Grix, 2001, 200), for which a combination of both quantitative and qualitative research would be more appropriate in order to understand the contexts in which these attitudes and opinions are formed.

In the UK, the broader research community appears to be lacking in researchers who have a firm grasp of quantitative methods, a fact reflected in the ESRC's – the largest funder of independent research in the UK – emphasis on this type of training for postgraduates. A research methods training course will have to show that it provides adequate training in quantitative methods, in order to obtain the sought-after ESRC

'Kitemark', whilst a budding social science postgraduate will have to show an aptitude for quantitative research to obtain a coveted postgraduate scholarship.

Qualitative research

Qualitative research is seen by many as almost the complete opposite of quantitative research. It usually involves in-depth investigation of knowledge through, for example, participant observation (as in anthropological fieldwork), employing the interviewing technique, archival or other documentary analyses, or ethnographic study (Ragin, 1994, 91). These methods do not rely on, but can involve some, numerical measurements. Qualitative researchers generally seek to amass information from their studies on, for example, a particular event, decision, institution, location, and issue, or a piece of legislation (King *et al.*, 1994, 4), with a view to discerning patterns, trends and relationships between key variables. This type of research involves the interpretation of data, whereby the researcher analyses cases, usually a few in number, in their social and cultural context over a specific period of time, and may develop **grounded theories** that emphasise tracing the process and sequence of events in specific settings (see Holloway, 1997, 80–87). Hence, in contrast to quantitative research, the researcher is not detached from, but positively interacts with, the object of study. Critics of this type of research point out that studies are usually small-scale and not generalisable beyond the case researched.

Qualitative research has enabled complementary research into such topics as the nature of dictatorships, by interviewing people who lived under such conditions and by uncovering the 'texture' of the relationship between the state and its citizens. It is unlikely that such 'rich' findings would be produced by statistical data alone. The aim for the new researcher is to weigh up and choose the best combination of possible methods to shed the maximum light on their chosen topic.

Ethnographic studies are generally qualitative in nature, for this type of enquiry usually requires the researcher to submerge him- or herself in the culture of a given society or group with the aim of finding patterns of power between specific group members, studying symbols of identity formation, and so on. Such a study usually entails a prolonged period of actually living in and among the group under observation, often befriending them and becoming part of their community. A full-blown ethnographic study is not always practical, given the time constraints of a modern PhD. Social science research is, however, full of in-depth case studies, which draw on many ethnographic research methods, whereby researchers spend up to one-third of their total research time undertaking work in the field. Another type of qualitative enquiry is sometimes called **thick description** (Geertz, 1973). Here, social phenomena are traced back to their origins in detail, by reconstructing specific events and using a wide variety of sources – which in some cases may be cross-checked with one another, or **triangulated** – to arrive at a plausible 'description' of the chosen subject of study. (The notion of triangulation in research will be revisited in chapter 4, when we will discuss the mixing of research methods and data, both in qualitative and quantitative research.)

The quantitative–qualitative dichotomy: a false antithesis
There are a number of issues in social science research that revolve around the quantitative–qualitative dichotomy. Figure 2 does *not* underline or subscribe to this dichotomy but rather shows how both types of research are often perceived among academics.

Quantitative	Qualitative
usually tackles **macro** issues	tends to analyse **micro** issues
employs a **deductive research** strategy	employs an **inductive research** strategy
is argued to be rooted in the **positivist** tradition	is said to be rooted in the **interpretative** tradition
is said to be **theory-testing** and predictive	is said to be **theory-generating**
aims to identify general patterns and relationships	aims to interpret events of historical and cultural significance

Figure 2: The quantitative–qualitative dichotomy

Figure 2 broadly sets out how both strands of research have come to be associated with certain types of enquiry in academia. There is no reason why one should not employ methods usually associated with quantitative research in an in-depth case study of a particular town, for example, undertaking a statistical analysis of variables pertaining to people who are most likely to vote in an election, their socio-economic status and newspaper-reading habits. Equally, methods usually associated with qualitative research are frequently employed in comparative analyses across cases, for example, using the interview technique to speak to political elites in a number of countries. As Blaxter *et al.*, point out, interviews, commonly associated with qualitative research, can be 'structured and analysed in a quantitative manner' and surveys, usually associated with quantitative research, 'may allow for open-ended responses and lead to the in-depth study of individual cases', or, in other words, a qualitative approach (1997, 610). As we shall see in chapter 4, methods can be mixed and indeed, in many cases, ought to be. The point of figure 2 is simply to flag up some of the different terms associated with the broad division in methods. In reality, this division is to some extent artificial, and the best research usually employs both methods (King *et al.*, 1994, 5). The key for new researchers is not to become entrenched in one or other camp, a sentiment I shall return to when discussing disciplinary boundaries. Hammersley, with whom many academics may not fully agree, neatly sums this up when he states 'the process of inquiry in sciences is the same whatever method is used, and the retreat into paradigms effectively stultifies debate and hampers progress' (1992, 182, cited in Silverman, 2000, 11). This is true to a certain extent. However, it must be said that academics with competing ontological and epistemological views would have problems with a universal 'process of inquiry' and may not believe 'progress' to be possible in social sciences in the first place.

You should choose your methods according to the questions you wish to ask. Whatever method you employ in your studies, you need to bear in mind that 'methods should follow from questions' (Punch, 2000a, 5), not the other way around. A poor question–method fit can lead to serious delays in research and, ultimately undermine your project. There are two key reasons for spending some time considering the question–method fit in your work. The first is that the questions you wish to ask should, to a great extent, guide your choice of methods. This is a logical research step that points you to a specific method of obtaining information. You will need to decide, after an extensive literature review (see below), which is the most appropriate method for your project and why the other methods used by the scholars you have read are not more suitable. Second, as Punch explains, by starting with the research question, you avoid what he terms '*methodolatry*, a combination of *method* and *idolatry* to describe a preoccupation with selecting and defending methods to the exclusion of the actual substance of the story being told' (ibid., 21). You need to bear in mind that methods are only tools with which researchers obtain information – unless, of course, your thesis is concerned with the nature of methods themselves.

Both the quantitative and qualitative paradigms, and the methods associated with them, have as their goal the making of inferences, that is, 'using facts we know to learn something about facts we do not know' (King *et al.*, 1994, 119). Whatever the method, the researcher needs to guard against misusing them. Ultimately, any method of enquiry in research can be manipulated (which amounts to cheating) to produce different results from those that the researcher would have had with the data he or she really collected. It is not for nothing that Disraeli once stated 'There are lies, damned lies and statistics'. Equally, imprecise details of interview partners and interview techniques, and of their relevance to the study, constitute bad scholarship. Manipulating information derived from interviews, especially those that are not recorded, or from any form of data collection, is dishonest and deceitful, but that will not prevent it from taking place. No one method is better than any other, but some methods are more relevant to your project than others. As I shall suggest in the next chapter, one way of avoiding false conclusions drawn from empirical data is to have more than one method of enquiry.

Methodology

The difficulty in understanding just what the term 'methodology' means has not been helped by the fact that it is used interchangeably with 'research methods' and is often considered, mistakenly, to be close in meaning to 'epistemology', 'approaches', and even 'paradigm'. Epistemology should be looked upon as an overarching philosophical term concerned with the origin, nature and limits of human knowledge, and the knowledge-gathering process itself. A project's methodology, on the other hand, is concerned with the discussion of how a particular piece of research should be undertaken and can be understood as the critical study of research methods and their use. This term refers to the *choice* of **research strategy** taken by a particular scholar – as opposed to other, alternative research strategies. The methodology section of a Master's or doctoral thesis, which is, especially in political science, often replaced with a section on 'ontology and epistemology', has come to mean 'the difficult bit' among students, through which they have to wade before being allowed to go off 'in the field' and enjoy themselves. A student's methodology is driven by certain ontological and epistemological assumptions and consists of research questions or hypotheses, a conceptual approach to a topic, the methods to be used in the study – and their justification – and, consequently, the data sources. All of these components are inextricably linked to one another in a logical manner. This is also the section that can take the most time, as students attempt to place their work among the canon of existing works on their topic, drawing on insights from wide-ranging literature reviews, and developing an 'innovative' angle on events.

Theory

In the social sciences, there appears to be a bifurcation of those who subscribe to the need for **theory**, conceptual devices or some form of abstraction to undertake research, and those who do not. Of course, the degree of complexity of any explanatory tool will depend on your discipline and your object of study. As always, there is a balance to be found between telling a story of an isolated case with no deeper understanding of the underlying processes of cause and effect, and overburdening the reader by stifling the content with elaborate theoretical considerations. Academic discourse, and the use of the term 'theory' in popular parlance, have added to the confusion of just what theory is supposed to be, because:

> Like so many words that are bandied about, the word theory threatens to become meaningless. Because its referents are so diverse – including everything from minor working hypotheses, through comprehensive but vague and unordered speculations, to axiomatic systems of thought – use of the word often obscures rather than creates understanding. (Merton, 1967, 39)

The first thing to remember is that you should not use theory for the sake of it. One common mistake in PhD theses is a lack of connection between the theoretical section, the purpose of which is to shed light on the empirical work, and the actual research undertaken, with the result that both sections could, in fact, stand on their own. The purpose of the theoretical part of a doctorate or project is precisely to give a sense of order to the empirical section, so that the two parts need to be inextricably linked; otherwise, you defeat the object of abstraction, which is to simplify and not complicate further the understanding of complex social phenomena. This does not, of course, apply to purely theoretical theses, which would have to be divided up somewhat differently. There is pressure on students to use 'theory' because it looks good, sounds sophisticated and indicates that you can get your head around the hard stuff. However, a 'bolted-on' theoretical section, which is not integrated or interlinked with the empirical section, is likely to end in a recommendation of a substantial revision of the thesis at the viva stage or, worse still, complete failure!

There is a certain hierarchy in explanatory devices on offer for use in research, not all of which are terribly complicated. Imagine a scale, where the starting point is the most abstract explanatory tool (theory) and the end point is the most straightforward (concept). In the middle lie a variety of incrementally more complex abstract devices to assist the research process. The list below sets out some of the most important explanatory tools available to researchers:

- theoretical or conceptual framework or scheme
- model/ideal type/typology/paradigm
- concept.

There is no general consensus on the role of theory in research. However, most social scientists attempting to *explain* complex social phenomena – as opposed to *describing* them in detail – agree that some form of framework is necessary to assist in selecting and prioritising certain factors over others and in showing relationships between certain concepts at an abstract level. Thus, by abstract connection of theoretical concepts *with observation*, the concepts gain in empirical meaning. This is why empirical evidence ought to be tangible, measurable or observable, as much theory in social science attempts to link observables with other observables, except, that is, those based on a 'realist' ontology, which seek to link unobservables with other unobservables. This simplification of reality is necessary if we are to achieve any kind of overview and weighting of certain variables and their effect on others. Gerry Stoker neatly sums up this concept by suggesting that theory:

> helps us to see the wood for the trees. Good theories select out certain factors as the most important or relevant if one is interested in providing an explanation of an event. Without such a sifting process no effective observation can take place. The observer would be buried under a pile of detail and be unable to weigh the influence of different factors in explaining an event. Theories are of value precisely because they structure all observations. (Stoker, 1995, 16–17)

Structuring our observations is vital if we are under both time and financial constraints. Postgraduates rarely have the luxury of simply gathering information and data in the hope of discovering specific patterns and relationships between phenomena. It is more likely that their ideas will already be informed by previous research and theories, discussions with peers and supervisors and 'gut' feelings which all help, at an early stage, to identify general research questions. Put simply, 'Theories are nets cast to catch what we call "the world": to rationalise, to explain and to master it. We endeavour to make the mesh ever finer and finer' (Popper, 2000, 59). Without theory, or at least some form of classificatory system, it would be extremely difficult to know which data and facts to collect in the first place. Even researchers setting out to generate theory from fieldwork have to start with some assumptions based on a certain level of abstraction. In the strictest sense, a theory consists of a 'system of statements that encompass a number of hypotheses or laws' (Schnell *et al.*, 1999, 52). Laws in this case relate more to natural science subjects, where tests are replicated again and again to produce the same results. There are very few instances of such laws in the 'messy' social sciences and humanities, as the study of people, their institutions, their environment and their creative output is a very complex task, and one which is made more difficult by the multitude of factors that go into making up social phenomena.

Another thing to note about theory is that it comes in many diverse forms, ranging from grand theory and middle-range theory to grounded theory (see Blaikie, 2000, 144 for a thorough examination of types of theory; and Marsh *et al.*, 1995, 17). Moreover, theories can be either deductive or inductive. Deductive theories 'arrive at their conclusions by applying reason to a given set of premises... For example, the rational-choice perspective in political science assumes that all political actors maximize their own personal utility, or self-interest, when choosing between alternatives' (Landman, 2000, 15). Inductive theories, on the other hand, arrive at their conclusions the other way around, by observing known facts 'on the ground' and then feeding them into a theory. In reality, most research uses both induction and deduction, as there is a necessary interplay between ideas and evidence in each research process (Ragin, 1994, 47).

The point here is not to give a survey of *types* of theory, but to highlight their significance in giving order and structure to the complex process of explanation, and ultimately, understanding. This is not to suggest that all students need a theory. As we can see from the above, there are several less complex devices with varying degrees of explanatory power that are suitable for social science research. Your choice of any of the examples given will depend on the nature of your topic and the focus of your study. One thing to remember is that it does not follow that using theory is far better than using a series of concepts specifically designed for your study.

Remember, too, that theories are, of course, bound up with certain ways of seeing the world, so you need to remain vigilant and on the look-out for interesting social phenomena which your theories may actually steer you away from.

Model, ideal type and typology

Gerry Stoker usefully differentiates between a theory, a **conceptual framework** and a **model**. All are explanatory devices, but at different levels of abstraction. The conceptual framework, like a theory, provides 'interpretations of relationships between variables' (Stoker, 1995, 18), but is less complex and has less explanatory power. It does, however, provide explanations and predictions for empirical observations. At one step down from a conceptual framework we have the model, **ideal type** and **typology,** which are less complex tools for comparing and classifying phenomena. A model is a representation of something, in the way that a model aeroplane is a replica of a real aeroplane. In social science, on the other hand, many academics attempt to represent reality by a series of boxes and arrows which depict and make explicit significant relationships between specific aspects of the model; thus a model 'enables the formulation of empirically testable propositions regarding the nature of these relationships' (Frankfort-Nachmias and Nachmias, 1992, 44). (The latter description of a model can be seen as a rather 'positivist' conception of research. Whilst I do not wish to subscribe to any particular type of research, I do find translating ideas into terms of boxes and arrows a very useful way of thinking through ideas.) Furthermore, a model, like theory, is an abstraction of reality, and a good way of visualising some of the relationships between concepts. In chapter 3 I will give some examples of hypotheses using models (i.e. boxes and arrows). The boxes and arrows themselves do not mean anything, except that they depict, in this case, the effect of one variable (let us say a person's dietary intake) on another (let us take level of fitness). If this relationship between two variables is written in text, the reader has to imagine it in his or her mind. By using a model, however, the reader receives an abstract picture of the relationship. This becomes more important when you add a list of other factors that may influence a person's level of fitness, for example, housing, upbringing, weight, etc. All of these influences can be schematically laid down to assist our thought processes. You are more likely to come up with other relationships, causal or otherwise, by using a model than if you attempt to store this information in your head.

The ideal type is, like theory, a construct that represents an intellectual description of a phenomenon in its abstract form. It should not be understood as an 'ideal' standard 'in the sense of being perfect, but rather that it is "ideal" in the sense of being an intellectual construct that may never exist in the real world' (Peters, 1998, 105). This confusion has arisen to a great extent because of the translation from the German (Blaikie, 2000, 165). Attributed to the founder of modern sociology, Max Weber, who was greatly influenced by economic modelling in his day (Weber, 1949, 89-90; Ringer, 1997, 110–21), an ideal type is a conceptualisation, such as, for example, the 'working class', with which the researcher can compare reality on the ground (empirical evidence). Ideal types are thus hypothetical constructs formed by emphasising aspects of behaviour and institutions which are empirically observable. These constructs isolate 'those variables central to the study of a problem, putting aside those aspects of the reality which seem inessential to the analysis' (Engerman, 2000, 258). An ideal type does not, however, posit relationships among variables. One could, for example, draw up an ideal type of successful post-communist political parties. You would need to ask the question 'why have some former communist parties been successful in some countries and not in others?' This initial question would guide the researcher's critical review of the literature (on selected countries, to make it manageable). Instead of reading everything ever written on post-communist parties, the researcher will be concerned with analysing the factors that have led to the success *and* failure of certain parties. In this way, an ideal type of a successful post-communist party can be drawn up.

You can see that this is only a yardstick or **heuristic tool** for analysis, for in such a simple model it is very difficult to factor in regionally-specific conditions and culture, differing types and extents of democratic transformation, and so on. Differences and similarities will allow the researcher to gain a deeper understanding of the specific contextual backdrops to a party's success or failure. If the researcher discovers certain patterns pointing towards success and failure across several examples, the ideal type could lead to further propositions in social science enquiry, for, although it is not a hypothesis as such, it could lead to the suggestion of fruitful hypotheses. Weber himself suggested that the 'ideal typical concept will help develop our skill in imputation in *research*: it is no "hypothesis" but it offers guidance to the construction of hypotheses' (Weber, 1949, 90). For example, an ideal type could suggest that if conditions A, B and C exist, we are likely to have or experience D. Thus, this type of construction is usually more abstract than a typology (see below) and refers to specific characteristics in institutions or people, such as Weber's well-known 'bureaucracy' and 'charisma'.

Our annoying conference hack, mentioned earlier, is an ideal typical construct. He or she exhibits certain characteristics – for example, always asking questions on ontology and epistemology – and possesses the ability to 'talk a good race', yet may well have produced few publications. Here, the analogy of a 'gym-fighter' springs to mind, that is, one who pounds the living daylights out of the punchbag in the gym only to crumble at the sound of the first-round bell in a real fight. In every department or institute in the country, usually in the canteen or common room, this ideal type is to be heard putting the world to rights. However, we must be aware that when using ideal types like this, we have to consider the possibility of a conference hack who exhibits all of the above characteristics, but who *has* published widely in an area different from that being presented at the conference. This type would differ from the first, and we would have to adjust our ideal type in the light of this empirical observation, or simply make a distinction between two ideal types.

Typologies are similar systems of classification to ideal types. They consist of 'a system of categories constructed to fit empirical observations so that relationships among categories can be described' (Frankfort-Nachmias and Nachmias, 1992, 40). These devices can be seen as loose frameworks with which to organise and systematise our observations. Like ideal types, typologies do not provide us with explanations, rather they describe empirical phenomena by fitting them into a set of categories. What they do help researchers with is the organisation of a wide range of diverse facts that can be structured into logical, but sometimes arbitrary, categories, which facilitates understanding of complex matters. Bailey sums it up thus:

> One of the chief merits of a typology is **parsimony**. …A well-constructed typology can work miracles in bringing order out of chaos. It can transform the overwhelming complexity of an apparent eclectic congeries of numerous apparently diverse cases into a well-ordered set of a few rather homogenous types. (1992, 2193, cited in Neuman, 2000, 44)

In comparative politics, the typology has a slightly different role. Built on the earliest classification scheme proposed by Aristotle, it serves to 'reduce the complexity of the world by seeking out those qualities that countries share and those that they do not share' (Landman, 2000, 5). In this case, the analyses are usually statistical and a typology can be seen as an initial stage on the way to theory-building (Peters, 1998, 95).

Paradigm

The common use in research of the term 'paradigm' draws directly on Thomas Kuhn, who depicts a paradigm as an institutionalisation of intellectual activity which, in effect, socialises students into their respective scientific community. Kuhn explains:

> By choosing [the term paradigm], I mean to suggest that some accepted examples of actual scientific practice – examples which include law, theory, application, and instrumentation together – provide models from which spring particular coherent traditions of scientific research.... The study of paradigms ... is what mainly prepares the student for membership in the particular scientific community with which he will later practice. Because he there joins men who learned the bases of their field from the same concrete models, his subsequent practice will seldom evoke overt disagreement over fundamentals. (1996, 10–11).

This is not dissimilar to what is usually termed 'an established academic approach' in which academics use a common terminology, common theories based on agreed paradigmatic assumptions and agreed methods and practices (see Rosamond, 2000, 192). Furthermore, paradigms are often overtaken, replaced or placed alongside other paradigms, leading to what is commonly called a 'paradigm shift'. In academic disciplines, dominant paradigms exist and are often challenged. In macroeconomics, for example, the neoclassical paradigm (or 'school of thought') and its world-view has, since the late 1960s/early 1970s, taken over as the dominant approach from its predecessor, Keynesianism. Both of these paradigms are based on specific ontological and epistemological assumptions which are reflected in the emphasis and priority they place on specific factors, although there is, of course, limited variation on these matters within both paradigms among protagonists. Whilst neoclassical economists advocate the virtues of an unfettered market and a small role for the state, Keynesian approaches usually call for a more active role of the state in stimulating the economy.

The use of paradigms in everyday research, however, should be limited to crude and broad groupings of certain approaches to the study of a specific topic – for example, on the collapse of communism, the academic literature can be broken down into 'top-down' and 'bottom-up' research paradigms. The former concerns itself with, inter alia, power-wielding elites, the latter with the role of citizens in the regimes' maintenance and collapse. The point is that you need some way of focusing and structuring your observations, otherwise you will end up writing an interesting story without being able to begin to differentiate, at least, between the way in which people approach a specific topic.

Concepts

Concepts are the building blocks of theory, hypotheses, explanation and prediction. A concept can be seen as an idea, or notion, expressed and compressed into one or more words. Concepts represent the least complex stage on our continuum of abstraction. That is not to say that concepts cannot be extremely complex. A concept carries with it a certain perspective and certain built-in assumptions, or ways of looking at empirical phenomena (Neuman, 2000, 44), and can be seen as an agreed-upon term among scholars. The agreement, however, is only on the term's existence and not its meaning, as much scholarly debate revolves around precisely this point. A concept is an abstraction of empirical phenomena based on certain assumptions, and can be used as a type of shorthand in explanation. For example, the concept 'book' 'assumes a system of writing, people who can read, and the existence of paper. Without such assumptions, the idea of *book* makes little sense' (Neuman, 2000, 44).

By way of demonstration, let us consider the concept cluster 'conditional loyalty', which I used in my own research to capture the relationship between the majority of citizens in the GDR (German Democratic Republic) and the GDR regime. This simple concept was used to suggest that the majority of citizens did not undertake any regime-threatening actions as long as certain 'conditions' were met. My aim was to trace the decline in this 'loyalty' over time and to give reasons for this, all as a way of contributing to an explanation of the regime's collapse (Grix, 2000). This short example reveals the work a single conceptual phrase can be made to do, and how much information can be packed into it. The key is to be as precise as possible – i.e. about what you mean by 'conditional', what exactly the conditions are and, of course, what the social, economic and political contexts are in which the action you describe is taking place. Operationalising concepts, that is, translating them into measurable variables for data collection, is one of the hardest jobs in research. This process is explained further in the next chapter, with reference to research questions and hypotheses with which to guide your research.

The abuse of concepts

Researchers must take care not to employ wrongly context-dependent concepts that have been developed at a specific point in time to describe specific phenomena. This can happen if an 'original' concept is referred to by an author, but without him or her actually revisiting the original texts to substantiate their claims and, importantly, without taking into consideration the changes that may have taken place in the world since the concept was introduced. Some further examples will illustrate this.

In the vast literature on the concept of 'social capital', by far the most dominant paradigm is the 'Putnam School' (referring to Robert Putnam, whose path-breaking work in 1993 did much to popularise the term), which unites a group of scholars who seek to employ Putnam's definition of social capital and, more importantly, though to different degrees, emulate the quantitative research methods used by Putnam to 'measure' the concept in his study of democracy in Italy (see Grix, 2001). This research paradigm has advanced our thinking on the concept of social capital and the social phenomena described by it, but has done so in keeping with the ontological and epistemological underpinnings of Putnam's own work. This paradigm also includes a growing body of work in which the term 'social capital', as used by Putnam, is frequently 'adopted indiscriminately, adapted uncritically, and applied imprecisely' (Woolcock, 1998, 196). The original definitions, indicators, methods and methodology used and put forward by these authors are often taken on, regardless of the changes in society and global governance that may have occurred since Putnam's works were written, and regardless of the refinements he has made in his subsequent research (Putnam, 1996; 2000). Examples abound where concepts and terms have been rendered hollow or extremely hard to define due to this overuse and abuse. Take, for example, the concepts 'stakeholder' and Albert O. Hirschman's schema 'Exit, Voice and Loyalty' which have, to a certain extent, suffered this fate (for the original theory see Hirschman, 1970; for a brief overview see Grix, 2000, 18–22). The use of 'stakeholder' in Britain, which was popularised by Will Hutton (1996; 1999) and the Labour Party, came to mean, among other things, giving a person a stake in society. The term was used so frequently, and in so many different situations, that its original meaning is now somewhat obscured. Albert Hirschman's 'Exit, Voice and Loyalty' scheme, which has been used in as wide a range of settings as social capital, was reduced simply to 'exit' and 'voice' in numerous explanations of the collapse of the German Democratic Republic. The original schema, presented by Hirschman in 1970, is rarely referred to, and the third pillar of the scheme, loyalty, is hardly discussed at all (see Grix, 2000, 21–2).

Another danger is for concepts to be diluted into a catch-all term like 'civil society', which is impossible to pin down, but regarded as somehow signalling something desirable. The concept of civil society is an interesting one, as it experienced something of a renaissance during the peaceful revolutions of 1989 that marked the beginning of the end of communism. However, the concept has been associated mainly with western capitalist societies, and simply extending the term to countries transforming from years of dictatorship to some form of democracy is not without its problems. Moreover, it can come across as prescriptive if western countries state that they will not assist these fledgling democracies until they have a functioning civil society, presumably based on the western model. This becomes particularly problematic when one considers the differences between countries and citizens who have had to live under dictatorial conditions. How can concepts developed in one cultural, political, economic, social and psychological context capture the complexities of, and be transferred to, another?

The point here is not to suggest that all concepts are context-specific and therefore of not much use outside the region or country for which they were developed. Far from it – the fact that it can transcend boundaries is the mark of a good concept and theory. The point is, however, to make you aware of the danger of *not* considering the origins of a concept (i.e. the context in which it has evolved) and the changes in society since the original concept was introduced.

Disciplines, discourses and interdisciplinarity

Academic disciplines are based on certain sets of ontological and epistemological assumptions, although within disciplines there is a wide variety of differing views among academics on which methods, theories, practices and concepts are the most suitable. Students need to be aware that each discipline, for example, sociology, economics, political science, has specific methodologies in which competing paradigms, consisting of common terminology and theories, coexist. At times it would seem that different disciplines speak a different language or discourse when describing the same event. It is important to know the constraints of particular disciplines, so as to understand that other types of explanation, whether they are theoretical or ontological in form, exist outside one's own field. Disciplines differ in the emphasis they place on the role and position of theory in research, with political science, especially American political science, stressing the need for theory and hypotheses in the pre-empirical stage, that is, *before* research begins. This is standard practice in American graduate schools and is seen as good, solid 'science'. An overemphasis on theory-building can, however, lead the researcher to lose sight of what it is they are meant to be studying. As with all stages of the research process, you must remain reflexive and willing to amend your pre-existing assumptions in the light of the previous or next stage of research.

Moving beyond one's own discipline, and its discourse, is to transcend the familiar: You can liken it to crossing national borders. For example, take a person who is happy to stay in Britain where he or she is familiar with the frames of reference, terms, terminology, signs, culture, social habits, language, tradition and his or her socio-economic place in that society. It is much easier for this person to remain in his or her familiar environment than to have to move to somewhere unfamiliar and learn all of the above from scratch. This may be transferred to the academic world by considering someone who remains strictly within disciplinary boundaries, a person who is not receptive to input from other disciplines. In this case, this person will deny themselves the chance of exposure to different frames of reference, terms and terminology, and different traditions and *Weltanschauungen* (world-views). They would be at a loss, for it is these experiences that we take back to, and which enrich, our own disciplinary training. (Incidentally, this unwillingness to 'travel' can also be the case *within* a discipline, for example, political science, where competing approaches to the study of politics coexist.) This is not to suggest that students ought to be proactively 'interdisciplinary', but rather that, by looking over and beyond disciplinary boundaries, researchers are often forced to reassess their 'taken-for-granted' assumptions – good practice in scholarship and a guard against disciplinary entrenchment.

'Interdisciplinarity' or 'post-disciplinarity'

The debate on interdisciplinarity is often very confusing, especially as the term itself is misused and lumped together with trans-disciplinarity, cross-disciplinarity and multi-disciplinarity. One way of thinking of the debate is to imagine a continuum which runs from multi-disciplinarity, where different scholars focus on the same area of study but remain strictly within their various disciplinary boundaries, to the utopian ideal of post-disciplinarity, in which no disciplinary boundaries are recognised, via transdisciplinarity, in which we all learn each others' trade. To paraphrase one well-known thinker: the last is a scenario where in the morning we do complex regression analysis, in the afternoon undertake some discourse analysis of literary texts and finish off the day assessing the use of the term 'totalitarianism' for capturing the key features of the Nazi dictatorship! The ideal of transdisciplinarity, and the loose manner in which the concept of interdisciplinarity is employed, are to be avoided, given the fact that it is hard enough for students to master the tools of *one* discipline fully in the short space of time afforded to studying at tertiary level (see Dogan, 2000, 98). It is better to speak of 'cross-fertilisation' between disciplines, whereby scholars learn from one another, share methods of research, and are willing to accept different interpretations of events. Equally, as Dogan rightly points out, using the example of his discipline:

> The relations between political science and the other social sciences are in reality relations between sectors of different disciplines, not between whole disciplines. It is not an 'interdisciplinary' endeavour…. The current advancement of the social sciences can be explained in large part by the hybridization of segments of sciences. (Ibid., 97)

The point of this section is to suggest that a willingness to look across disciplinary boundaries, and to learn and readjust our own points of view, is beneficial to scholarship as a whole. For it is at these junctures, that is, at the areas of overlap between the disciplines, that inter-disciplinary exchange, or a dialectic between disciplines, takes place. The aim is not the knitting together of disciplines in a seamless mass of interpretation and explanation, but rather the sharing of insights, best practice and methods with other disciplines. There is less a need for specific training in a range of different disciplines, than an open state of mind when approaching research.

Summary

This chapter has been concerned with the pre-research stage, outlining some of the most important things you should know *before* you begin your research. The major point I have attempted to get across is that familiarity with the tools and terminology of research is essential if you are to complete successfully a high-quality, precise, piece of work. Of equal importance is the ability of the researcher to pick and choose *which* methods, theories or conceptual tools to use for their particular project. If you do not know or understand what is on offer, you are unlikely to make the best choice. To sum up the advice of this chapter:

- Reflect on, and be aware of, the nature of academic disciplines and the range of ontological and epistemological assumptions guiding approaches within them
- Take time to learn the 'tools of the trade' (use the glossary at the end of this book)
- Familiarise yourself with the central concepts you are likely to come across in research, in particular, methods, methodology and theory (and other conceptual abstractions)
- Reflect on the concepts you are using in your research. Consider their origins and whether they are suitable for the context in which you wish to employ and defend their use. Avoid at all costs the 'abuse of concepts' outlined above

Further reading:

Blaikie, N. (2000) *Designing Social Research*, Cambridge, Polity Press.

Bryman, A. (2001) *Social Research Methods*, Oxford, Oxford University Press, chapter 1.

Engerman, S. L. (2000) 'Max Weber as Economist and Economic Historian', in: Turner, S. (ed.) *The Cambridge Companion to Weber*, Cambridge, Cambridge University Press.

Honderich, T. (ed.) (2001) *The Philosophers. Introducing Great Western Thinkers*, Oxford, Oxford University Press. An excellent brief introduction to philosophers and their thinking.

King, G., Keohane, O. and Verba, S. (1994) *Designing Social Inquiry. Scientific Inference in Qualitative Research*, Princeton, Princeton University Press.

Kuhn, T. S. (1996) *The Structure of Scientific Revolutions,* Chicago/London, University of Chicago Press.

Marsh, D. and Stoker, G. (eds.) (1995) *Theory and Methods in Political Science,* Basingstoke, Macmillan.

Neuman, W. L. (2000) *Social Research Methods. Qualitative and Quantitative Approaches,* Boston, Allyn & Bacon, 4th edition.

Punch, K. F. (2000) *Introduction to Social Research. Quantitative and Qualitative Approaches,* London/Thousand Oaks/New Delhi, Sage.

Ragin, C.C. (1994) *Constructing Social Research. The Unity and Diversity of Method,* Thousand Oaks, Pine Forge Press.

Silverman, D. (2000) *Doing Qualitative Research. A Practical Handbook,* London/Thousand Oaks/New Delhi, Sage.

3 Getting started

Introduction

Having been introduced to factors that will enable you to prepare the ground to begin research and after a whistle-stop tour of some basic tools and terms of the trade, you are now ready to make a start. There are various ways of deciding on a topic of study and this chapter will offer examples to help you focus your initial thoughts. The most common of these, the *literature review*, is given special attention, as everyone has heard of it but not everyone knows exactly what it is for, and *all* theses or dissertations will have to engage with a body of existing scholarly work. By dissecting the literature review and looking closely at its constituent parts, the aim is to make clear its central purpose in research.

Closely interwoven with the literature review is the process of devising research questions and hypotheses. Although these terms are more common in social science, the underlying *principle* is the same for many subjects in the humanities. As we have already seen, the purpose of arriving at a more precise research question is to give your study some kind of order and to assist you in narrowing down your topic to something that is manageable within three years. This time restriction is tough, but it can be very good for disciplining our thoughts. This chapter deliberately goes over in detail the terms and terminology associated with hypothesis building. Again, this is not to advocate a specific type of research or epistemology, but rather to help you understand what is meant by terms such as 'independent variable'.

The final section of this chapter introduces the units and levels of analysis used in research and the various *types* of research you can adopt (e.g. case studies; comparative studies, etc.). Once again, these are specific terms given to activities that go on every day without being thus labelled. If, for example, a student undertakes a thesis on a specific writer, this

would constitute an in-depth case study, providing that more general conclusions are drawn. Units and levels of research are simply technical terms
for the 'who' or the 'what' – and at which level (broadly, individual, group
or institutional) – we are studying. This distinction is important when the
researcher starts mixing analyses of individuals and institutions, for, as I
will discuss below, findings from one unit or level of analysis cannot
straightforwardly be extrapolated to a different unit or level of analysis.
Whatever choice you make, it will have a profound effect on the methods
you will use to get at your data. After you have undertaken a literature
review, defined your research questions and decided on the unit, level and
type of analysis, you will be in a position to think about **fieldwork**, a
subject dealt with in chapter 4.

All in all, this chapter should go some way in revealing the inherent *logic*
of the research process, indicating how the various stages of research are
connected and how researchers need to *reflect* on this interconnectedness
throughout their studies.

Getting started

The selection of a topic for study will be governed by certain criteria,
including the expertise at your host institution, *your personal interest*, and the
project's feasibility, that is, the need for the project to be realistic and manageable in the time available. The emphasis here is on *your* interest in a
topic, because *you* will be the one dealing with it on a daily basis for three
years. However, the first experience of actually having to narrow your
focus will probably come with the writing of a thesis proposal, when you
apply to an institution or a funding body. This is a very handy exercise in
the art of refining and defining exactly what it is you intend to do. It also
gives you a rough 'map' to follow in your studies (for an in-depth look at
how to construct research proposals, see Punch, 2000b). Do remember,
however, that original proposals rarely closely resemble the end-product,
as research is a to-and-fro of ideas, concepts and data. Here are ten points
that should be included in a good, clear research proposal:

1. The context of, and rationale behind, the project (i.e. set the scene
    and tell the reader *what* it is about by presenting them with a brief
    background to the topic and setting out your aims).
2. A brief literature review (indicate how the work you propose fits in
    with current scholarly debates).
3. The methodological approach you will adopt (here you need to give

some idea of the theoretical approach you are using) and how your angle on events fits in with the scholars discussed in (2).

4. Research questions and hypotheses (*what* exactly do you wish to find out, or what question do you hope your work will provide an answer to? Research questions should also point to the level and units of analysis you will use, and the generalisability of the conclusions sought – see the section on case studies below for more information on this).

5. Your methods of enquiry (in other words, *how*, or by which means, are you going to gather and analyse data? Make sure you indicate how this method sheds light on the questions you have posed).

6. The sources to be employed (what kind of sources are you drawing on?).

7. The significance and utility of the research (i.e. *why* is your research such a wonderful idea?).

8. Any logistical and other difficulties you envisage, and the means of overcoming them.

9. The specific research training required to undertake the project.

10. The timetable of the research.

By setting out the above in great detail, you are well on the way to starting a doctorate. Rarely, however, are the topic or questions contained in an initial research proposal 'sharp' enough for actual research. It is a good idea at this point to be as precise as possible, as questions which are too vague will not help you navigate the mass of possible information awaiting you. Although there are no hard and fast rules on how to arrive at a precise, narrowly defined and focused statement or research question, there are four very general techniques for helping to refine and focus your initial idea into an achievable and manageable project. I reiterate at this point that the advice of choosing a topic as soon as possible is driven by a sense of pragmatism, and not by any ideological or epistemological preferences.

1. The most common way to begin a large piece of research is by undertaking a literature review (sometimes called a literature search), which enables you to 'get a feel for the state of the art' on and around your general topic. It also allows you to assess the feasibility of your project and narrow your likely focus (see the literature review section below for typical sources to draw on).

2. Another way to start is by setting out research questions or hypotheses (for manageability, restrict yourself to three or four), a process which in

itself will lead you to the field of study and the correct methods for carrying out the research, including the type and level of analysis necessary, for example: systemic, institutional or actor-centred. Bear in mind that research questions should 'contain within themselves the means for assessing their achievement' (Blaxter *et al.*, 1997, 35). If your questions do not do this, then they are more than likely too general, and need to be sharpened.

3. By refining the key concepts you are employing in your project, you are forced to compare and contextualise. You will thus need to consult the relevant literature to 'place' and compare your concepts with those used in wider academic debates.

4. Another way to get started is to try to sketch out a research proposal or outline on the lines of that proposed above, and ask yourself such questions as 'What might the whole project look like?' and 'How will the thesis eventually be organised?'

You could, of course, mix and match each of the techniques listed above. This is probably what happens in the majority of cases.

The literature review, research questions and hypotheses

Let us consider further the role of a literature review, the best-known, yet least-understood method of starting a project. Reviewing the secondary literature on a given topic area is common to all theses, whether in the social sciences or humanities. The first thing to note is that reviewing the literature is not a compartmentalised stage of research. Instead, you should *constantly* review the literature until the day your thesis is submitted, by which time the last thing you want to hear about is a newly published study on a relevant topic. The review serves many purposes and is done in many stages. I suggest that there is a continuum which begins at one end with the initial 'dip' into the academic literature and ends, in the period shortly prior to submitting your work, with a 'checking' or 'skimming' of the literature. These two extremes represent two different reasons for reviewing the literature. As you move along the continuum from the initial literature review to the 'skimming' stage, the purpose of the ongoing review changes. These broad stages are discussed further below. Apart from getting you started on your research project, other reasons for reviewing the literature include helping to:

- focus and clarify your research problem (Kumar, 1999, 26)
- expose you to, and enable you to demonstrate a familiarity with, the approaches, theories, methods and sources used in your topic area (this is usually a prerequisite of a thesis and a key theme of the viva to which examiners will turn)
- highlight the key debates, terms and concepts employed in your topic area
- acquaint you with the sum of the accumulated knowledge and understanding in a given field and around a particular question or topic, otherwise known as the 'cutting edge' of research
- assist you in identifying a 'gap' in this literature, thereby justifying your particular study's contribution to research, and assisting in your choice of approach and methods
- contextualise your project within a wide-ranging existing knowledge base
- make you an expert in the field of your choice as part of your academic development.

In a literature review you must, above all, make reference to, and engage with, the key texts in your chosen field or on and around your topic. Before you can do this, however, you need to know *where* to look for the literature to review. There is a vast number of places to find literature, including the standard academic sources such as library catalogues and abstracts, CD-ROMs, dissertations and theses, back issues of relevant scholarly journals (both 'hard copies' and Web-based) and specific documentation centres. So much is now available in this area, and so rapidly are things changing, that it is advisable to get advice from specialist librarians whose job it is to guide users through the maze of complex bibliographical sources. Remember, with Web-based sources you need to note the Web address and the date you downloaded the information. Much of the material on the Web can not be used for academic purposes, unless it is linked to a recognised journal, dictionary, encyclopaedia (e.g. the *Britannica*) or institution. In addition, there is the relevant secondary literature in scholarly monographs (that is, a detailed study of a single subject) or multi-authored books.

Once you know why you are undertaking a review and where you can locate it, it is time to turn to the 'how'. Three crude stages of the ongoing literature review can be summed up thus: the initial 'dip', the 'hypothesis or research question' stage, and 'the critical review' stage. In between all of these stages, you must find time actually to read whole articles or books, as students under any type of pressure (be it temporal or financial) naturally try to cut corners. An additional type of literature review is the so-called 'skimming' technique, which you can only really undertake once you are already very familiar with a topic and have grasped the core assumptions, arguments and debates contained therein.

The initial 'dip' (stage 1)

At the very start of a project, the best thing to do is undertake an initial review of the academic literature, guided by the 'hunches' you have already or by sheer interest in a topic. During this stage, your 'gut' feelings will be quite quickly confirmed or corrected, which will assist you in gradually acquiring knowledge of your subject, and, more importantly, if it is done correctly, it will give you a broad overview of what has been written already. There is no point in setting a specific time limit for this stage of the review, because everyone works at different speeds and has differential access to material. Suffice it to say, you ought to agree with your supervisor on a set period of time to undertake this stage. Ideally, six to eight weeks of uninterrupted searching and reading should be sufficient for you to obtain an *overview* of the relevant literature in your field. A good idea is to ask an experienced academic who works in your field for some tips regarding literature. After consulting your supervisor, you could even seek advice by e-mail from someone you do not know personally, as some are happy to help research students, especially those who are copiously citing their work. Academics' addresses, e-mails, and so on can usually to be found in your relevant association's directory – for example, the *Political Science Association/British International Studies Association Directory* has contact details of people in politics and international relations in the UK (the same principle applies to most disciplines: simply locate your key association, consider joining it – it usually brings benefits – or visit the association's Website). Or, if you know someone's academic affiliation, it is usually easy to find their e-mail address from their university's Website. Try to get them to guide you to the key texts or articles, including their own work, that you should read. What are, generally speaking, the key debates and approaches to the subject in your field?

Once you have located, photocopied or obtained the key literature around your topic, you can set about reading it. You should, even at this early stage, attempt roughly to organise the literature according to different approaches, methods employed and overall conclusions. Once you have consumed the literature you have collected, you are ready to move on to the next stage in the review and in the research process: hypothesis building, or generating research questions.

'Second' literature review, research questions and hypotheses (stage 2)

Before embarking on a full-scale search of everything that has ever been written on your topic, you need to find a way of narrowing your focus. The best way to do this is to go through a process of developing 'hunches' or ideas into research questions and/or hypotheses to guide your work.

There is no agreed way of arriving at a research question or hypothesis, but most researchers are convinced you do need one to begin the research process (Pennings *et al.*, 1999, 6). Your own interest, ideas, previous research and personal experience will have led you to the academic field on which you wish to concentrate. The initial literature review would have assisted you in selecting a broad topic for study within that field. Now you are ready to set out a *proposition* about your chosen area of study. Although this, again, may seem to fall in with the 'positivist' research design I discussed earlier, the intention is to assist you in narrowing your focus at an early stage. Do be aware that proceeding this way does not imply that you must *restrict* your overall research focus, for you can adapt and firm up your questions and propositions later in the research process.

In the social sciences in particular, it is considered increasingly necessary for a research question or hypothesis to relate to, and be important for, 'real-world' phenomena (King *et al.*, 1994, 15). In both the humanities and social sciences, the research question should show how it makes a contribution to an existing scholarly literature. Therefore, if we take German foreign policy as our example of an area of interest, we could pose the question within this huge subject: 'Will German–Polish relations be important for the further integration of the European Union (EU)?' You need to decide whether you wish to use a research question to guide your work or a more abstract tool, a hypothesis. Do not insist on using hypotheses when a specific research question would do. Both of these tools will assist the research process by guiding your reading in a full-scale literature review, and by helping you select methods and particular sources. It is very important at this stage to decide how you will formulate your research problem, as the latter is 'like the foundation of a building. The type and design of the building is dependent upon the foundation' (Kumar, 1999, 35).

A hypothesis is different from a research question in as much as it is usually more closely linked to a theory, and will posit the answer to a research question within itself, which will subsequently be 'tested' in fieldwork. The choice of which to use in a study will be governed by the type of study you wish to undertake; for example, a simple research question will suffice for a descriptive study. The research question above could be formulated in a hypothesis, if this were appropriate and if you wished to *explain* rather than describe. From the literature on European integration, you would have repeatedly read about the 'Franco-German motor' as a central force in bringing Europe closer together, i.e. the close and fruitful bilateral relationship between two former enemies, Germany and France. Thus, at this early stage, you could posit the tentative proposition – or hypothesis – that good German–Polish cross-border relations will have a positive impact on future European integration (just as Franco-German friendship did). A hypothesis states a relationship between two, or more, concepts and suggests that one has an impact on the other. Verma and Beard sum up a hypothesis and its role in research as:

> A tentative proposition which is subject to verification through subsequent investigation. It may also be seen as the guide to the researcher in that it depicts and describes the method to be followed in studying the problem. In many cases hypotheses are hunches that the researcher has about the existence of relationship between variables. (1981, 184, cited in Bell, 1993, 18).

The concepts in the hypothesis need to be *measured* in some way 'in order for the hypothesis to be systematically tested' (Bryman, 1995, 6). To convert concepts into measures, often called the 'operationalisation' of concepts in research, the researcher develops variables, which can be understood, simply, as concepts that vary in amount or kind. There are no set ways of finding suitable variables for hypotheses (Bouma and Atkinson, 1995, 53), as there is no set way of arriving at a research question or hypothesis in the first place. You need to be aware that such a measure 'is likely to be a relatively imperfect representation of the concept with which it is purportedly associated, since any concept may be measured in a number of different ways, each of which will have its own limitations' (Bryman, 1995, 7). There is a danger, that by constructing hypotheses, you gain direction, specificity and focus on the one hand (Kumar, 1999, 64), but on the other, they may divert your attention away from other, potentially interesting, 'facets of the data' that you have collected (Bryman and Cramer, 1994, 4).

Returning to the example of a hypothesis above, we can now set it out as follows (although, in general, researchers would not use a diagram for a simple two-variable relationship; (Neuman, 2000, 56)):

This simplified hypothesis states that there is a positive relationship, indicated by the plus sign, between the concepts 'German–Polish cross-border relations' and 'European Integration'. In this uncomplicated example, the box labelled 'German-Polish cross-border relations' is sometimes referred to as the **independent variable** (shown as 'X' in formal models). It is also known as 'a causal variable, an explanatory variable, an exogenous variable, or the explicandum' (Landman, 2000, 17), or the thing that 'causes' something else – in this example, European integration. The latter, sometimes depicted as 'Y' in formal models, is termed the **dependent variable**. Other terms for this include 'outcome variables, endogenous variables, or the explanandum' (ibid., 16), or simply the thing which is 'caused' by the independent variable. It is important to be aware that every dependent variable can be an independent variable, or vice versa: it is the *researcher* who decides where to place the emphasis. Your proposition does not need to be set out as above, but, as I have suggested, schemes and diagrams using boxes and arrows help us visualise the relationships we seek to explore. As a research guide, the above hypothesis is too broad, but what it does do is narrow your reading further and pose a number of important questions which will impact on how you proceed with your work: for example, which type of German–Polish cross-border relations? Over what period? What do you mean by integration? and so on. This helps you find answers to these questions by returning to the relevant literature you used for your initial 'dip'.

A further exploratory literature review could result in unpacking the following debates or strands of research:

- works covering *formal* German–Polish relations at inter-governmental level (bilateral)
- works discussing relations between border regions (e.g. in one of the so-called Euroregions along the German–Polish border)
- *informal* relations (e.g. cross-border flows of people, goods and ideas)
- the variety of disciplinary approaches to this topic, ranging from international relations and political science to area studies and geography.

From this breakdown of literature on and around our example, three broad areas of research can be distinguished, under the first three points of the list above. The next task is to focus further still on the area you wish to study by sharpening the hypothesis in the light of your literature search. The period of study has to be manageable, so for this example, you could select one specific type of relations and a five-year period, leading to the following hypothesis:

The period of study is now 1996-2001 and the **working hypothesis** – that is, a provisional conjecture to guide the investigation which will be refined in the light of further reading and research – is that increasing informal cross-border co-operation contributes to European integration.

Full-scale critical literature review (stage 3)

After the revision of your hypothesis, you are ready to undertake a thorough review of the literature, which will enable you to:

- become further acquainted with the literature on your chosen topic
- gain insight into the key debates and major questions on informal cross-border German–Polish relations
- confirm your initial hypothesis or hunch that 'X' has a positive impact on 'Y'
- learn how other, more experienced researchers analyse the subject and which theories, methods and sources they employ
- sharpen and narrow your focus of enquiry further to particular types of informal relations and
- reassure yourselves that there is not already a wealth of literature positing exactly the same hypothesis.

As I have mentioned before, you need to see the literature review as an ongoing, reflexive process, just like the whole research process itself. By this I mean that the constituent parts which make up the literature review and the whole doctorate are *constantly* revisited throughout the period of study. You need to consider each and every stage of the research process in the light of the preceding and subsequent stage and the way one impacts on, or connects with, the other. The critical literature review outlined above, is, however, crucial to the beginning of research, as it sets the parameters for your project.

Doctoral students have to locate their approach vis-à-vis other scholars in the field, and they have to justify why their chosen approach is better suited to the task than any other. A good way of achieving this, and structuring your first chapter, is to set out the review according to 'different approaches, interpretations, schools of thought or subject areas' (Blaxter *et al.*, 1997, 112). There are many benefits of such an approach. It not only sets up the argument in the light of other researchers' work, but also shows the reader that you are very well aware of the range of literature in your field. The critical reading of works dealing with your chosen topic also has the benefit of drawing attention to their strengths and weaknesses, allowing you to 'position' yourself against the rest, to offer some further justification for the approach chosen, and to indicate to the reader your take on events.

You should avoid developing a 'thinly disguised annotated bibliography' (Hart, 2000, 1) in the place of a proper, and critical, review of the literature. The purpose is to engage with the current literature, and to use it to develop your own approach and argument by critically analysing and flagging up the ideas you find fruitful or not. You should be looking to 'note any controversies in this literature, explain their origins and evolution, detail the arguments made by both sides, and summarize their current status' (Van Evera, 1997, 101). You should not be presenting the reader with a giant book review, simply regurgitating in the form of a synopsis the contents of each book you have laid your hands on. A structured approach as outlined above can give order to the array of diverse literature available on your topic (see Hart, 2000, 10), which can range over a wide variety of disciplines and discourses and include different types of text, from serious academic monographs or journalistic accounts to 'officially' produced material of firms, associations, political parties, and print media.

After undertaking a literature review with the revised hypothesis in mind to discipline your reading further, you can now return to the drawing board and redefine your proposition. By now, you will be aware of the key approaches in your respective fields or areas of study. At this point, you should reflect on the appropriateness of the mainstream approaches for your questions and projects, and you should not shy away *from developing different approaches* or a mix of different approaches, drawing on different variables to test your hypotheses. Here, the importance of having a hypothesis will become apparent, for in order to choose the most appropriate approach or theoretical framework to organise the data, you need to be clear about the 'what' and 'why' questions. In the example, I have chosen German–Polish relations and European integration (the 'what'), and narrowed this down to informal cross-border flows as my independent variable, or the thing which causes or contributes to European integration in the hypothesis. Thus, I need to decide on the exact types of informal cross-border relations to study and find a way of measuring their impact on the integration of the region. I also need to explain what I mean by integration, which might in this case be the 'sense of community' (Deutsch, 1957) in and around the border region which leads to further economic, political and social co-operation between two societies. Basically, I need to establish whether an increase in informal cross-border relations has been accompanied by a cognitive shift in co-operation and understanding between the population of the two states. Put another way, I wish to analyse whether increasing cross-border co-operation impacts on people's perception of the 'other' and assists in overcoming historical legacies that stand in the way of co-operation. If this can be established, then I could suggest there is a correlation between 'increasing German–Polish informal relations' and European integration (i.e. X impacts on Y). As you can see, once you start to unpick the question or hypothesis, it has a whole number of implications for how you are going to attempt to answer, validate or refute it (for a thorough discussion on refuting or 'falsifying' hypotheses see Popper, 2000, 27–48 and Bell, 1993, 70). The next stage of research is inherent in the question or hypothesis you are posing: what *level* and *unit* of analysis are you going to use? And what *type* of approach and *method* of empirical research will you choose?

Levels and units of analysis in research

How do you set about answering a research question or hypothesis? You need a research strategy, an umbrella term which covers the following:

- the manner in which you approach your research topic, for example, inductively or deductively
- the research questions or hypotheses
- the level and units of analysis
- the type of study

- as a consequence of the preceding factors, the sources of data to be collected with which to answer, validate or refute your hunches.

The research strategy is often referred to as a framework for analysis, something that will give structure to the enquiry and make you think of methods of **data collection** and sources. Closely linked to methods and sources are the indicators – or variables – that you need to select in order to get at your questions. 'Hard-nosed' social scientists – that is, those rooted in positivist philosophy of social science positions – would insist that such variables are measurable, tangible or at least observable, so that the researcher can record them properly. However, it is important to remain aware of the potential role of those factors that are not so easily measured: for example, the effect of tradition, the concept of trust, and the influence of social context on actors' behaviour, etc. At this point, you need to consider carefully how other researchers have operationalised concepts and 'measured' things in your field. As I suggest below, it is preferable to have a variety of 'hard' (quantifiable) and 'soft' (less easily quantifiable) indicators to:

- allow yourself the best chance of actually getting at the information you want
- prevent an all-out attack on your methodology by the examiners in the viva (unless, that is, you want to mount a clear defence of your methodology and how it leads to a choice of specific variables to oper-ationalise.)

The level of analysis on which you focus will be linked to the units of analysis you choose. Units can include individuals, groups, organisations, and social categories and institutions (Neuman, 2000, 134), the exact choice of which will impact on the methods and sources used in your study. The thing to remember with units of analysis is that each has 'unique attributes; thus it is often misleading to shift from one unit to another. 'Generalizations based on individuals as units of analysis and generalizations based on groups can be quite different' (Frankfort-Nachmias and Nachmias, 1992, 53).

It is possible to mix units of analysis, but you need to distinguish between them in the study and remain aware of their relationship with the level at which you are operating. In this way, you will avoid a mismatch between units, that is, attempting to explain something on an individual level by drawing conclusions from findings relating to aggregate data, in other words, a different level of analysis. In research methods textbooks this is referred to as the 'ecological fallacy', but has little to do with tree-hugging and environmental preservation (Neuman, 2000, 136). Adopting different levels of analysis in the same case study can, however, offer a richer account of a specific event by employing different 'lenses through which to view phenomena' (Robins, 1995, 69), which are based on different assumptions. As a consequence, 'the level of analysis determines what evidence is considered permissible and hence guides the fieldwork process and underscores the way in which the data are ultimately interpreted' (ibid., 69). Two common levels of analysis in social science are the:

- micro-level, individual or actor-centred
- macro-level, system or structure-centred.

A straightforward study of why individuals vote for a particular political party could focus on the individuals themselves, asking them, by way of a questionnaire or interview, why they voted for party X, Y or Z. If, however, you wished to include an analysis of how particular parties attract voters, your analysis would have to shift to an organisational level. There is no problem with including all sorts of levels of analysis in your study, sometimes called a 'multi-level analysis' (Pennings *et al.*, 1999, 9), as long as you distinguish clearly throughout your work the level at which you are operating.

In much social science, there appears to be a divide between those scholars who 'believe all of politics can be explained by focusing on micro-level processes' and those who 'believe that all of politics can be explained by a focus on macro-level processes' (Landman, 2000, 17). The debate about whether to focus on structure or agency in research touches on a much wider, and unsolvable, ontological puzzle in social science which has become known, simply, as the **structure and agency problem** (see Hay, 1995). For example, if you are looking to explain the behaviour of a relatively small number of individuals, you will no doubt be better off actually speaking to them or sending them a detailed questionnaire. If, on the other hand, you are looking to explain the role of a certain institution in governing or influencing the behaviour of individuals, you will be presented with a more difficult task. Not only will research on the evolution of the institution itself be necessary, but you will have to delve into the structure–agency debate. Briefly, and simplistically, this dilemma revolves around the puzzle of whether it is the social context in which individuals act that guides and determines their actions, or whether it is the individuals (or actors) themselves who form and shape the social context and institutions around them. As always, it is probably a bit of both. However, it has become customary in political science to establish a position on this, especially as up and down the country in various academic forums the question 'Where do you stand on the structure–agency debate?' is frequently asked. This makes the task of, for example, assessing an institution's impact on actors' behaviour, or actors' input into the development and evolution of institutions, extremely difficult. If you are trying to explain social phenomena, however, you should at least attempt, to some degree, to ascertain the direction of causality in your study.

Deciding on levels and units of analysis

Returning to our hypothesis on Polish–German informal cross-border relations and their impact on European integration, the next thing to do is to decide on the level and unit of analysis. You could, on a simple level, take the amount of certain transactions between the two states as an indicator of interaction and see if, over the five-year period, this has led to deeper institutionalisation of informal relations. Here, you could go a step further and propose that the institutionalisation of relations would assist Poland's pre-integration into the EU by bringing it into line with existing EU member structures. For such a study, you would need to understand both the *volume* of flows between the countries and their impact on people's *opinions* and *attitudes* to each other. Therefore, one unit of analysis could be economic transactions and the other could be the opinions and attitudes of the population. The former is operating at the macro level, the latter at the micro. In this case, the units of analysis have pointed us to the types of methods and sources needed to go some way to validating or refuting the hypothesis.

It is clear that cross-border flows as an indicator lend themselves to quantitative research and opinions or attitudes to a more qualitative approach (the latter is only true if you were researching a specific target group and not a large-scale survey of the population, however). Thus, the example given would need a mixture of both quantitative and qualitative methods.

Statistics alone are unlikely to tell us everything about the attitudes of the residents of two opposing sides of any border region towards their neighbours, and interviews alone are not reliable enough for tracing the levels of cross-border flows over the five-year period. Thus a mixture of methods and sources (such as questionnaires, documentary analysis, newspaper articles, statistical documentation from economic institutes, elite-level interviews and their transcripts) are needed to get at the complex issues set out above. With this in mind, you are in a position to return to the working hypothesis, to refine it and to make it more sophisticated before beginning further reading and fieldwork, that is, the collection of empirical data (or 'reality') against which you will check your hypothesis. The central hypothesis now proposes that transnational exchange in the form of cultural networks, social transactions, information flows, people, ideas, and so on, generates a healthy stock of mutual trust, which in turn has a positive effect on the integration of Poland into the EU.

All of these terms and concepts will need to be fleshed out in a proper PhD, but the intention of this example is to illustrate that this refined hypothesis is your 'map' to your fieldwork. In a real research situation, you would need to be aware of the wider questions and forces of causation, for example: What is the relationship between formal and informal modes of cross-border relations? Is the former a prerequisite of the latter? By pointing to relationships between other variables, this example would gain in explanatory power and generalisability, i.e. it could be used in other settings. Before you can embark on your fieldwork, or the collection of empirical data, however, you need to consider the following: the type of study and the units and levels of analysis on which you are going to focus.

Types of study

There is a variety of types of study available to the researcher and the choice will, once again, relate directly back to what it is you want to know, what you think it is possible to know and what there is to know about (i.e. your ontological position). Long before you embark on fieldwork, you will have to decide on the type of study you wish to undertake. The most common types are the case-study approach and the comparative approach. Case studies are by far the most popular form of study at doctoral level and are necessarily included in analyses that compare cases, usually across countries. Broadly speaking, there are three types of case study (Yin, 1994, 1):

- descriptive
- exploratory
- explanatory.

The first generally applies to a thesis with a more historical subject. Its aim is not to explain the influence or impact of certain factors in the event on which it is focusing, but to give a detailed account of a particular issue, person or process. An exploratory case study, on the other hand, is usually carried out with the intention of either testing initial working hypotheses, checking for availability of, and access to, relevant data, ascertaining the relevant variables for a study and assessing the suitability of the case for further, more extensive, research. A mini-exploratory case study is usually a good idea for doctoral students, because you need to be sure you are asking the right questions, have chosen the correct case to study, and are likely to have some data with which to answer your questions, before you commit yourself to a long period of fieldwork. The explanatory case study is perhaps the most common in the social sciences, in which researchers seek to make generalisations by extrapolating the single case study's findings to other cases (see below).

Yin, the most cited writer on the topic, defines a case study as an 'empirical inquiry that investigates a contemporary phenomenon within its real-life context, especially when the boundaries between phenomenon and context are not clearly evident' (ibid., 13). The emphasis on context is crucial, as the rationale for honing in on a specific case is to be able to identify, uncover and unpick specific contextual factors in which the event, person or policy you are analysing is embedded. Once you have decided that the case-study approach is the best way forward, you need to ask yourself whether a single (in-depth) case study is suitable or maybe a series of case studies, referred to, simply, as a 'multiple-case' study. Single, in-depth case studies are increasingly the format many PhDs theses are taking, which is fine providing students display an awareness of wider theoretical and methodological issues. A single case study is a very specific approach to phenomena 'through thorough analysis of an individual case' (Kumar, 1999, 99). The subject of such a case could be anything from an individual, a town, a group or political party, a region or community, a specific process, decision or policy, and so on. Case studies are not tied to any particular research method and they are not 'methods' themselves, but instead should be seen as simply an organisational strategy, within which social data are organised 'so as to preserve the unitary character of the social object being studied' (Goode and Hatt, 1952, cited in Punch, 2000a, 150).

To assist in deciding whether a case-study approach is best for you, look carefully at the manner in which experienced researchers in your field have set about their analyses, whilst bearing in mind that the aim is to produce something original and distinctive. It is very common for students to begin their studies with more case studies than they end up completing. Remember, if you are not undertaking a comparative study, it is better to do one case properly than to skim over five or six without being able to probe deep enough to uncover anything worthwhile. In the social science community single case studies have tended to be looked down upon, chiefly because of their lack of generalisability, though this objection is no longer made as strongly as it once was. Punch offers positive reasons why single cases are valuable:

> The first is what we can learn from the study of a particular case, in its own right ... the case being studied might be unusual, unique or not yet understood, so that building an in-depth understanding of the case is valuable.... Second, only the in-depth case study can provide understanding of the important aspects of a new or persistently problematic research area.... Discovering the important features, developing an understanding of them, and conceptualizing them for further study, is often best achieved through the case study strategy. (2000a, 155–6).

One in-depth case study of a relatively under-researched area can be embedded in, and compared with, the existing body of literature and studies to gain useful insights into a particular region or to establish similar patterns between well-researched regions and the chosen study. In-depth studies are also capable of contributing to the advancement of specific theories (Ragin, 1994, 46), especially if local or regional specificities can be shown to have relevance for, or to be similar to, causes and effects inherent in incidences or events beyond the territorial limits of the original case study. Researchers must be careful, however, not to 'immerse themselves wholly in the case study details' (Blaxter *et al.*, 1997, 66), but must instead ensure their study is embedded in, and connects with, a wider body of academic research.

It goes without saying that the type of case study you choose will impact greatly on the methods you employ and the data you collect. If, for example, you do an in-depth study of a particular town, analysing the role of civic engagement in facilitating local democracy, you will be able – in the course of three years – to speak to the majority of civic leaders who matter, to local councillors and to other town dignitaries. To supplement your elite-level interviews, you could analyse the relevant articles on participatory politics in the local press and gather statistics relevant for the town (e.g. How many people use their right to vote? How many people take part in extra-parliamentary action and how often?). Here you can see it would appear relatively easy to collect the data necessary for covering such a topic in a single town or region. To add even more value to such a study, although this is not always necessary, it would be good to do exactly the same for a different town, which perhaps has a similar history (let us say both towns used to be busy harbours), but which, in contrast with the other, flourishes economically. By dipping into the research toolbox discussed in the previous chapter, you can set about categorising why town A fares better than town B and what impact, for example, levels of civic participation have on local economic growth rates. Try repeating the above example over ten cases and you would be in trouble, first, intellectually, as local, social, economic and political contexts differ so much that such a wide comparison would be hard to maintain, and second, financially, as such an exercise would demand considerable resources. You cannot possibly interview 500 people in addition to gathering supplementary information. The time required to set up, and carry out, let alone analyse, that amount of interviews, will take you way beyond the temporal limits of doctoral research.

Comparative studies

Most comparative research textbooks emphasise the fact that people compare things on a daily basis, as they set about distinguishing between sizes ('big', 'bigger') and types ('different', the 'same'). It is very hard, if not impossible, to undertake any form of quantitative or qualitative research without resorting to some sort of comparison, because most of our judgements are checked against previous experience and knowledge which we bring with us to the research situation. Whilst this intuitive comparison takes place constantly, 'comparative studies' can be seen as a specific *type* of study, especially within political science. The rationale behind comparative studies can be understood as the following (based on examples in Landman, 2000, 4-10):

- to provide contextual knowledge about other countries, their systems of governance, and so on. By comparing, the researcher places his or her own country or system in a wider context, whilst drawing out similarities or differences between countries produces further information and knowledge
- linked with the discovery of similarities or differences, the notion of classification, touched on in chapter 2, whereby the comparative researcher attempts to arrive at a typology of countries, electoral systems, welfare states, and so on.

The final two, interlinked, reasons behind comparative studies are:

*   hypothesis testing
*   prediction.

The former consists of developing a hypothesis to be tested in cross-comparison analyses, something deemed by some as a prerequisite for the starting point of any comparative study (Pennings *et al.*, 1999, 6). The latter is the harder job to undertake – the researcher attempting 'to make claims about future political outcomes' (Landman, 2000, 10) based on generalisations derived from a comparison of several countries.

Comparative studies have to involve more than one case, by definition, be it the same subject for study across time or a number of separate subjects. Comparison can take place on a case-by-case basis, for example, using in-depth studies to compare French drinking habits with those of the British, or both countries' welfare systems (fieldwork for the former may be more interesting than the latter!). Cross-national comparisons usually involve the researcher measuring variables across a number of nations. Indicators such as GNP (gross national product) or statistics referring to births, deaths, age, etc., are converted into variables and analysed using statistical analysis. If your comparison is to be cross-national and you intend drawing on sources other than statistics, you need to think seriously about language, as you would be, in effect, interpreting the interpretations of others. Relying on scant English language coverage is not ideal as a source base for a doctorate. The level of written and spoken language competence needed for a PhD will depend very much on the type of study you undertake and the methods you employ.

In summary, comparison, according to Pennings *et al.*, can be seen as:

> one of the most important cornerstones of the development of knowledge about society and politics and insights into what is going on, how things develop and, more often than not, the formulation of statements about why this is the case and what it may mean to all of us. In short, comparisons are part and parcel of the way we experience reality and, most importantly, how we assess its impact on our lives and that of others. (1999, 3)

As suggested in the last chapter, typologies are frequently used in comparative research as a tool with which to compare cases. Typologies are often derived in the first instance from comparing a variety of cases, noting the chief characteristics and listing them. It is this list which can be used as a sort of device with which to study further cases. Without labelling it as such, most academics categorise, classify and sort out the information they have gathered, in order to compare it and, ultimately, to make sense of it.

Summary

This chapter has been concerned with the 'getting started' stage of research, perhaps one of the hardest for first-time researchers. The key aim has been to reveal the inherent *logic* of the research process, but also, to show its *reflexive* nature. To sum up:

- Research is not a linear process developing in clearly differentiated stages from beginning to end, rather, the researcher must remain reflexive throughout the whole process.
- The core components of a doctorate, however, are linked in a logical way.
- The literature review is an ongoing process which can be (artificially) divided into three stages: the 'dip' stage, the 'hypothesis or research question' stage and the 'critical review' stage.
- You should use research questions or hypotheses as guides to your reading and research, but remain aware of those factors from which they may point you away.
- Regardless of whether you study three cases in one town, or three towns in one country, or whether you compare one country with three others, you need to be aware of how the *type* of study you are doing links with the *level* and *unit* of analysis you choose and the degree of generalisability of your conclusions. You need to justify and defend your views on this.
- Importantly, you need to make sure that these types, levels and units are the correct ones to shed light on the research questions you wish to answer or the hypotheses you aim to validate or refute

Further reading

Blaxter, L., Hughes, C. and Tight, M. (1997) *How to Research,* Buckingham, Open University Press.

Bouma, G. D. and Atkinson, G. B. J. (1995) *A Handbook of Social Research. A Comprehensive and Practical Guide for Students,* New York, Oxford University Press.

Hart, C. (2000) *Doing a Literature Review,* London, Sage.

Hay, C. (1995) 'Structure and Agency', in: Marsh, D. and Stoker, G. (eds.) *Theory and Methods in Political Science,* Basingstoke, Macmillan. Still the best and most accessible introduction to this debate.

Kumar, R. (1999) *Research Methodology. A Step-By-Step Guide for Beginners,* London/Thousand Oaks/New Delhi, Sage.

Landman, T. (2000) *Issues and Methods in Comparative Politics. An Introduction,* London/New York, Routledge.

Pennings, P., Keman, H. and Kleinnijenhuis, J. (1999) *Doing Research in Political Science. An Introduction to Comparative Methods and Statistics,* London/Thousand Oaks/New Delhi, Sage.

Punch, K. F. (2000a) *Introduction to Social Research. Quantitative and Qualitative Approaches,* London/Thousand Oaks/New Delhi, Sage.

Punch, K. F. (2000b) *Developing Effective Research Proposals,* London/Thousand Oaks/New Delhi, Sage.

Yin, R. K. (1994) *Case Study Research. Design and Methods,* London/Thousand Oaks/New Delhi, Sage, 2nd edition.

4 Methods, fieldwork and stages of research

Introduction

In chapter 3 we discussed the range of factors that researchers need to consider before deciding which methods to employ in their studies. This chapter will assist this process by outlining some of the key methods of empirical data collection and by suggesting how they may be combined in a given research design. I have deliberately avoided discussing the full range of methods of data-collection and analysis, including, for example, statistical analyses, as the latter are very specialised, and an in-depth text should be consulted before adopting them (for example, see Pennings *et al.*, 1999). The point here is briefly to introduce methods common to many postgraduate studies, namely different types of interview techniques, questionnaires, participant and non-participant observation, and certain types of documentary analysis. This section is rounded off by a discussion on mixing methods and the notion of triangulation in research, something that students should consider. It also warns of the danger of using too many methods at the expense of depth.

The subsequent section offers advice on preparing for fieldwork. As with the section 'Before you start' in chapter 1, there are a number of things you need to think about and plan in advance. One key factor is access to materials, people, organisations and institutions. It is no use setting off on fieldwork without a clear list of people to meet and places to go, otherwise you will spend half the time available to you locating them.

The final section recaps on all the steps of the doctoral process that we have discussed so far and includes a diagrammatic overview to assist understanding of how the parts of research link together. By demonstrating the interconnectedness of the stages of research, it is easier to understand why the researcher must remain *reflexive* throughout. In addition, a table of research stages, specifically designed to represent the three years of doctoral study, is provided to show approximately what you should aim to achieve at certain points during the 36 months of study. If you wish to build up a portfolio of employment-related skills during your studies, you need to make the most of the opportunities that may arise at different points throughout your doctorate.

Methods: different types of enquiry

This section highlights some of the most common research methods used in gathering and analysing empirical data *in the field* and comments on their key characteristics. In addition, there follows a brief introduction to questionnaires, because they are frequently employed alongside interviews and in some cases produce very similar data. This is not an exhaustive list of the myriad methods on offer and you are advised to consult a book on research methods for further, and more specific, information relevant to each method. The list below is not presented in order of preference, complexity or usefulness. You need to think carefully through your research questions before selecting a method with which to seek to answer them. The short description of methods in this book is intended to assist in this process.

Although humanities students may not use the terms employed in this section, they do use, directly or indirectly, many of the methods outlined below. It may not be possible to interview Goethe and ask him his opinion on certain matters, but it may be possible to interview a Goethe specialist and gather information in this way. In any case, the discussion below is not discipline-specific and is relevant to researchers who intend using any of the methods discussed.

Interview technique

The interview is a very popular method in doctoral theses, especially elite interviewing, and for this reason more space is given over to it. Four broad types of interview technique can be used: the structured, the semi-structured and the unstructured interview, and group interviews (or focus groups, as they are sometimes called). Interview data can be collected either quantitatively (except for unstructured interviews) or qualitatively. Before introducing the interview method, some general points should be made:

1. It is usually wise *not* to use interviews as the *sole* method in your study, but rather to apply them in conjunction with other methods of enquiry. Looking at the same phenomena from different angles will ensure a more balanced approach to your object of study and will probably shed more light on it.

2. Is interviewing really for you? Are you the right type of person to be interviewing? If the thought of meeting (important) strangers feels you with dread and brings you out in a cold sweat, then this is probably the wrong method to choose, though this will clearly have implications for your thesis topic and research questions.

3. The biggest problem students have with interviews is access to individuals, companies or institutions. This is something that needs to be thought about as soon as possible after beginning your studies. Writing to, and receiving a reply from, prospective interviewees can be a very lengthy business, something to factor into your research plans.

4. Find out exactly how much time the interviewees will have for you, so you can arrange the interview accordingly.

5. Always give yourself plenty of time to get to where you are going, as you certainly do not wish to keep people – usually very busy people – waiting, and you do not want to arrive at the interview sweating and puffed out. Make sure you have done your homework and found out where the interview is actually taking place (Grant, 2000, 7).

6. Make sure you have the correct equipment with you (including more than one pen) and that you are very familiar with your recording technology, as you and your interviewee do not want to waste time at the beginning of the interview fumbling about with equipment. If you are recording the interview (which, of course, you ask and obtain explicit permission to do) the best piece of equipment to use is a mini-disc recorder for perfect sound quality. Otherwise a good quality dictaphone will suffice. Whether to record interviews or not is a decision you need to consider. Interviewees tend to be more open and specific off the record, but this makes referencing the source and recording the interview somewhat more difficult.

7. Listen to and analyse your recording(s) or notes as soon as possible after the interview, in order to get the clearest picture possible of what has been said and have the best chance of clarifying any omissions in your notes 'while the interview is still fresh in your mind' (ibid., 2000, 14).

Structured interviews

The structured interview, as its name suggests, is the most rigorous and the least flexible in the way it is set up. Predetermined questions are put to the interviewee in a specific order and the responses are logged (either by recording electronically or by note-taking). The same process is repeated with a number of other interviewees and the results or findings can be compared with one another, categorised according to specific questions and aggregated statistically. Usually, interviews are carried out by the researcher, face-to-face with his or her interviewee. However, the structured technique can be also carried out via e-mail or by telephone (Kumar, 1999, 109). In this situation, interviewees receive the same prompt from the interviewer and there is not a great deal of digression from the script or interview schedule. The questions asked are usually 'closed', i.e. the interviewee has only a fixed number of answers and data resulting from the answers can be coded and processed easily (Bryman, 2001, 107–8). This technique is very close to survey questionnaires on which answers to predetermined questions are written in specific sections instead of given orally. The key aim of structured interviews is to achieve a high degree of standardisation or uniformity, and hence ease of comparability, in the format of answers. The drawback is that this technique is inflexible and is not designed to cope with the unexpected. On the plus side, you need fewer interviewing skills than are necessary for the unstructured interview – and even the semi-structured one – because in this situation you have a 'map' to guide you – a fairly rigidly drafted question sheet. It is this device that ensures a relatively uniform delivery of questions and prompts. On the negative side, you may miss the opportunity of discovering important information owing to the inflexible nature of this type of interview.

Semi-structured and unstructured interviews

One step down from the structured interview is the semi-structured, or in-depth, interview, in which you, the interviewer, have in mind a number of questions (you should not exceed ten in total, for manageability) that you wish to put to interviewees, but which do not have to follow any specific predetermined order. The advantage of this, perhaps the most popular method of interviewing, is that it allows a certain degree of flexibility and allows for the pursuit of unexpected lines of enquiry during the interview. The results and findings of such an interview can still be compared, contrasted and even converted into statistics. An unstructured interview, on the other hand, is one in which the researcher has a random list of concepts or loose questions, which he or she converts into spontaneous questions during the interview. Another, relatively popular, version of this is the so-called 'oral history' interview, in which open-ended questions are put to interviewees, who are actively encouraged to talk about their own biographies and to 'recount aspects of their lives and/or the lives of their contemporaries' (Blaikie, 2000, 234). This technique can be helpful at the very beginning of a project, as unstructured sessions can open up avenues of investigation, including informal discussions, previously unthought of. However, the answers and data gathered from such sessions are not comparable, as the content of each interview is likely to be very different.

Group interviews or focus groups

Group interviews usually involve the researcher and a specific group of people, for example, from a particular age cohort (youths), socio-economic background (the working class) or ethnic background. These type of interviews can also be structured, semi-structured or unstructured and recorded in the same ways as one-to-one interviews, that is, either quantitatively or qualitatively. Your role as researcher is, however, different inasmuch as you now act as a 'moderator or facilitator, and less of an interviewer' (Punch, 2000a, 177). The idea is to spark a dialogue between group members guided by topics supplied by you, and not to hold a traditional interview on a one-to-one basis.

Interviewing has many advantages, especially if you are aware of the pitfalls of relying solely on the data produced from them. They can provide information that is not printed or recorded elsewhere, and interviewees can assist in interpreting complex documents, decisions or policies. Also, interviewees, especially at the elite level, can provide you with further contacts. This is sometimes called the 'snowball' technique (Grant, 2000, 3), whereby you ask, specifically, whether the interviewee could name any useful contacts, thus allowing you to get in touch with important people using the interviewee's name and without having to resort to 'cold calling'.

Questionnaire or survey technique

Questionnaires are most effective when used in conjunction with other methods, especially one or more varieties of the interview technique. Put simply, a questionnaire is a list of questions sent to specific individuals, who then, if you are lucky, respond. It is vital that questions are clear, unambiguous and easy to understand (Kumar, 1999, 110). If a respondent misunderstands a question only slightly, their reply is very likely to be of little value to you and they are less likely to respond in the first place. If a number of your respondents understand a question differently from each other, their answers will be difficult to compare. Remember, unlike in a face-to-face interview, you will not be at hand to explain anything to the respondents, who must rely on the information in front of them. This may be an advantage, as there will be no 'interviewer effects' on the answers, that is, your personal characteristics, be they your socio-economic background, gender, etc., will not affect the respondents' answers (Bryman, 2001, 130). Try to avoid leading questions, or questions which tend to leave only one option open to respondents. Questions on sensitive matters should be preceded by a brief summary, 'explaining the relevance of the question' to the study (ibid.), giving the respondent some context to it. The questions should follow each other in a logical order (you should take great care to avoid unintentional duplication and arrange questions in the correct sequence) and should be set out in a user-friendly manner. This type of method requires careful consideration and is best undertaken only after you have developed a clear, precise idea of what it is you want to study. If you do decide to employ this method, you must consult a relevant textbook, attend a proper course or, preferably, both.

A good way of combining questionnaires with interviews is to have a separate question on the questionnaire sheet asking if respondents would be prepared to be interviewed at a later date. In this way you will have access to, and be able to mix, quantitative and qualitative data.

The response rate of questionnaires will differ widely. The obvious aim is to get back as many as possible. However, there is a general method-ological problem here, as it is likely that those who do not respond to your questionnaire are different from, or hold different views to, those who do. As long as you are aware of this potential bias, you can use other methods and data to correct it.

The observation technique

There are two basic types of observation technique: participant and non-participant. The first of these has been touched upon in chapter 2, with reference to ethnographic studies. This is the chief technique of data col-lection for ethnographers and anthropologists, who submerge themselves in the culture, customs, norms and practices of the people they are studying. One of the aims of being actually among the subject of inves-tigation is to understand how everyday life is conducted (Punch, 2000a,

184), by discerning specific patterns of behaviour, gestures, use of language, symbols and tradition.

Many researchers will use some form of direct observation, not necessarily as intense as that described above. By noting down and categorising what you observe, you are recording snapshots of empirical phenomena. For example, you may take part in a form of direct political action like a social movement or demonstration. In explaining how such an event came to take place you would need to draw on other works analysing the factors that motivate participation in the first place, as being present at an event does not guarantee you will gain a clear understanding of this. Again, as long as you remain aware of the pitfalls of extrapolating from unique incidents, and as long as you link your findings to the wider literature on this subject, such direct observation of unfolding events can prove invaluable. However, for exciting revolutions and political coups, you are unlikely to be in the right place at the right time. Seriously, securing access to observe people, groups, etc., can be difficult, and even if you do gain access, you need to ensure that your presence does not unduly affect the action of others in their 'natural setting'. Some researchers structure their observations much in the same way as an interviewer does in a structured interview. They have a notion of what they should be looking for and how they should record the findings. The findings can be used for quantitative analysis, in the same manner as the data produced by structured interviews.

Non-participant observation usually involves a passive role for the researcher, who does not directly influence events, but observes interaction, which, it is assumed, is unaffected by the researcher's presence. For example, a researcher may observe the interaction between a child and its mother or a group of children playing, taking notes or even videotaping the scene (on how to take fieldwork notes see Neuman, 2000, 363–6). Videotaping gives you the option of going over and over the 'original' data analysing modes of interaction (Blaikie, 2000, 233–4).

In the literature there is a general distinction between structured and unstructured observation, which centres on the issue of either going into the field with particular categories, concepts or classifications in mind or not. Unstructured observation is characterised as an approach out of which classificatory systems and patterns emerge. As with many components of research, you can, of course, combine the two by starting with loose categories which you adapt in the light of unstructured observation. This distinction, and the possible combination, is not unlike the discussion of inductive and deductive theory in chapter 3. The debate is about the extent to which the researcher interacts with empirical data, applying or modifying preconceived concepts, notions, expectations and assumptions. There is a thin line between using conceptual tools as a means of guidance and being over-reliant on them, ending up with tunnel vision, failing to notice or deal adequately with phenomena outside the reach of the conceptual tools used.

Documentary analysis

Documentary evidence comes in all shapes and sizes, ranging from official and private documents to personal letters or memos. To some extent all theses engage with specific texts or documents. The level at which this is done can range from the full-blown and technical discourse analysis to simply reading texts with the aim of gaining information of a person's or organisation's viewpoint or policy. This type of analysis will point you to very specific sources, in this case written documents or texts. You must consider carefully the origins and authors of these documents or texts, the purpose they were originally written for and the audience they were intended to address. In addition, you have to distinguish between *primary* and *secondary* document sources, with the former usually considered those that have arisen as a product of the actual research process and the latter as interpretations of events by others (Bell, 1993, 68). For example, if you record and transcribe your interviews, these could be considered primary sources. If, on the other hand, a second researcher uses your transcriptions for their research, they would be using secondary sources. This is not a very good idea in reality, given that they were not present at the original interview and are thus analysing the record of a conversation. That record has been recorded and interpreted (from tape to text) by you.

The archival technique

Archives vary a great deal across a wide range of different source materials. However, a few general points can be made about using this method. First, as with interviews, you need to secure access at a very early stage in the research process: for example, in Germany there is a waiting list of approximately one year to view the files of the former secret police (the 'Stasi'). This has obvious connotations for a doctoral student who, at a relatively early stage, needs to have thought through and decided upon exactly which archival files he or she intends to use. The next step is to contact the archive in question and arrange dates when you can visit. A good idea, if possible, is to make an exploratory visit, checking the content of the archive (scouring the indexes of files) narrowing down and selecting the material you wish to order. The guides, catalogues, referencing systems and rules on photocopying vary tremendously from archive to archive (see Vickers, 1997, 174).

Archival sources should be, by definition, secondary, as they are usually dated and have been recorded by someone else. However, unearthing such sources and employing them for the first time in a research project renders the primary/secondary distinction difficult to uphold. The chief aim of using this type of method is to bring 'dead' documents alive to shed light on specific events, personalities or policies by introducing them to a wider readership. You must take care, as with all data gathered, not to simply select the documents or files that support your hypotheses, for the latter may be *refuted* and not just verified.

Finally, a word or two on the archivist who is assigned to you. The role of the archivist is not to be underestimated, and it can be a matter of luck whether or not you end up with one who is sufficiently interested in your project. But luck can be given a helping hand by courteous and professional treatment of archivists – at a minimum, punctuality and acknowledgement of assistance is essential. There seems to be a relationship between the interest an archivist shows for your project and the type, amount and quality of data you will receive. Under normal circumstances you should obtain most of the standard documents listed in a catalogue. If, however, you chance upon or can cultivate a keen archivist, you may be lucky to find that there are many relevant files that are not listed in the sections that you have been wading through.

Documents

All documents have been written with a purpose in mind, are based on particular assumptions and are presented in a certain way or style. A political party's manifesto or regular documents for dissemination are a case in point. A trade union will also have a particular angle on events, as will a think-tank or an association linked to a political ideology. The researcher must be fully aware of the *origins, purpose* and original *audience* of any document before researching it. In this way you can analyse the documents in the context in which they were written. This method of data analysis is often linked to **hermeneutics**, an approach which seeks to analyse a text from the perspective of the person who penned it, whilst emphasising the social and historical context within which it was produced (Bryman, 2001, 382–3). For example, an internal memo from one level of government to another in a dictatorship may shed light on how the centre maintains power and the way in which information feeds back into the system of control. This document may, on the other hand, say more about the individual sending it than the system as a whole. Other documents may have been phrased in a certain way to appease superiors, when in fact what they were reporting was a distortion of the truth, as was the case with the official 'feedback' mechanisms (i.e. the secret police) in many former communist countries. The best guard against biased findings is to use other methods or sources to complement the documents you have collected.

Documents made public which clearly state a party's, association's or organisation's aims and objectives can be used as a very good benchmark against which you can measure on-the-ground reality. A housing association, for example, may state that their central concern is investment in social housing to empower local residents to engage in local activities directly related to where and how people live. You might analyse these documents and perhaps speak to a few key individuals in the association and build up a succinct list of their intended aims. Now you have a resource from which you can construct a questionnaire or interview questions to 'check' against reality in fieldwork. If the association's aims and objectives can be measured statistically – for example, crime rates, attacks, and so on – this could be used to complement the above techniques of data collection.

Discourse analysis
A more sophisticated form of document analysis is discourse analysis. This technique, increasingly borrowed by the social sciences from linguistics, studies the shifts and turns in the use of language over time or in particular usage, often in the form of a micro-analysis, for example, where the researcher identifies active and passive verbs, and so on. Social scientists have discovered this technique and are employing it to get at such tricky or 'slippery' concepts as identity. For example, social constructivists in the field of international relations, leaning on work undertaken in sociology, draw on discourse analysis to understand the way in which identities, ideas and institutions interact and impact on each other. At its most complex, this type of analysis uses special software packages to deduce patterns and changes in language use by examining, electronically, a database or corpus capable of storing millions of words. The latter can be described as 'The collection of computer-readable language that you assemble for your project [and] selected on the basis of your research criteria' (Barnbrook, cited in Hoffman and Knowles, 1999, 28).

Print media
Print media, especially newspaper articles and reports, are a popular

source in doctoral research. They can be a useful complement to interviews and statistics. If you are undertaking an historical study, newspaper reports can give you a 'feel' for the views and opinions of the printed press, or the wider opinions they represented at that time. A more up-to-date study may indicate and inform you of wider sentiments in the country you are studying, for example, British attitudes to European Monetary Union (EMU). You need to be fully aware that the media landscape is very broad and represents a wide range of diverse interests. Thus an analysis of the *Daily Mail* with respect to the EMU question may not give you a comprehensive picture of people's actual attitudes towards Europe. Therefore try, as far as possible, to alleviate obvious bias by using two or three newspapers with different political allegiances. It is particularly important for a researcher working in a foreign country to be fully informed of, and knowledgeable about, that country's print media to be able to make and ultimately justify their choice of newspaper sources.

Print media can be a useful source for academic research, and most organisations and political parties produce something in written form. If you are undertaking content analysis, that is if you are interested in the amount of attention paid to a particular event by the print media, you may wish to do a quantitative analysis of reporting in one specific newspaper over a certain period of time. Alternatively, a qualitative approach might mean having to find out who compiles the reports or articles, who is the target audience and under what conditions they were written, as a Chinese 'underground' newsletter is likely to be written in a different style, to say, *The Times*. Interestingly, in analyses of newspapers, for example, one can discover certain patterns or emphases of reporting on particular topics, or indeed a change in topics and themes themselves over a period of time. This can be carried out in either a quantitative or qualitative research strategy. With the introduction of CD-ROMs, researching back-copies of newspaper editions has become much easier. You can now type in keywords, for example, 'The Third Way', and retrieve all articles in the past year or more on the topic, count them, download them and begin the analysis. This is an excellent way to get a quick overview at the beginning of your studies.

Triangulation: mixing methods and data

Now we have an idea of some of the most common research methods used in postgraduate work. It is nearly always best to try to use more than one method of enquiry to improve your chances of getting better, more reliable, data and to minimise the chance of biased findings. Using more than one method in research is sometimes referred to as triangulation. This term is derived from navigation, military strategy and surveying, which, according to Blaikie (2000, 263–70), is misleading and has led to the popular conception that triangulation simply means approaching an object of study from different angles using different methods. He points out that triangulation is, in fact, very difficult, chiefly because of the different onto-logical and epistemological underpinnings of research strategies, consisting of combinations of methods, which are used. Here I re-emphasise that methods themselves should be viewed as mere tools for collecting data. They should not be looked upon as being automatically 'rooted in epistemological and ontological commitments' (Bryman, 2001, 445), even though academics and their disciplines often forcibly uphold the notion that certain methods are inextricably bound up with specific world-views. In other words, as long as you are aware of *how* you are employing a specific method, and *how* this relates to the ways in which you employ other methods, there should be no problem.

Method and data triangulation

When speaking about triangulation in research it is important to differ-entiate between a number of factors that can be triangulated. Method triangulation is a process in which the researcher uses two or more research methods to investigate the same phenomenon. This can be done either sequentially, that is, one method after the other, or at the same time. In most studies it is not possible to use more than one method at a time, so that a sequence of stages of research emerges. It is among these stages, and the various methods used, that checks and balances between data can be made. For example, you might first undertake in-depth qualitative interviews and follow this up with a questionnaire that could be used for statistical analysis (see Neuman, 2000, 125).

On the other hand, data triangulation is a process in which the researcher uses multiple sources of data, a process similar to that used in some comparative analyses where the same object of study is analysed using a number of different measures or variables (Peters, 1998, 97). An example of cross-checking data which have been collected using different methods is the comparison of interview transcripts with published documents, or statistics derived from a local investigation which are compared with other, national, statistical sources for accuracy (see Robins, 1995, 72).

If we disregard the semantics of the word 'triangulation' and concentrate on what it has come to mean in social science, the best summary would simply be that it *is* about observing an object of study from different angles. The major benefit for the researcher, and scholarship in general, is that findings or conclusions are 'likely to be much more convincing and accurate if ... based on several different sources of information' (Yin, 1994, 92). Thus, the best advice for students is to attempt to check findings derived from one type of method with those derived from another, as long as the original fact under investigation remains the same, thereby enhancing the validity of their study. However, beware of falling into the trap of using various methods superficially, skipping between methods because one does not seem to bear the results you were hoping for (see Silverman, 2000, 99).

Fieldwork

The previous chapters have set out the things that you need to be aware of before developing a fieldwork plan, and the previous section has given a quick overview of some of the most popular methods of data collection. This section suggests some factors to consider when compiling a fieldwork plan and before setting off to collect any data. A careful fieldwork plan will enable you to carry out data collection without wasting time and energy and head off the danger of gathering huge quantities of unworkable information. Before drawing up a fieldwork plan, you should be quite clear on the following:

- the precise topic
- the methodological approach being used
- the project's research questions or hypotheses, and the level of analysis and the methods by which the data is to be collected.

Now you need to set about deciding *where* you are doing your fieldwork and contacting relevant individuals and institutions. This initial brainstorming should include thinking about:

- accommodation for the period of fieldwork, which will usually be away from your place of residence
- a list of contacts and institutions where you are going to research
- a list of various sources to be collected – and their locations
- the names, addresses, full contact details (telephone, fax, e-mail) and affiliations of people to be interviewed.

Fieldwork needs to be planned well in advance, especially if you are meeting high-profile people who have very busy schedules. At this stage it is useful to produce a chapter outline for the thesis as a whole: this will be provisional, of course. However, you do need to think through which direction your studies may take, and the outline provides you with a 'map' while you are doing your fieldwork to remind yourself exactly why you are there. This mental process helps you to imagine, and thus be in a position to respond to, what might happen, as more often than not something will crop up in the field which will affect your original plan of action. This technique is often used in sport, for example, competitive running, in which success requires a psychological focus as well as a particular level of fitness. What sorts the wheat from the chaff among equally well-trained athletes on race day is the ability to *think* they can win, or improve. They *envisage* in the mind's eye a number of scenarios of what might happen during the race, and prepare for them.

The relevance to fieldwork is obvious: if you go to archive X and the source you are relying on turns out to be very thin on the ground, you need a contingency plan. For this reason the collection of data (if you are not undertaking an ethnographic study, where the emphasis is on a long stay in the field) is best done in several stages. This allows an initial feasibility study to see if access to material is possible or, indeed, if the material you need actually exists. A second, fuller, field trip would ideally break the back of data-gathering, with a subsequent trip to mop up loose ends or conduct some final interviews. One of the most important points here is that students often get too involved in their immediate surroundings on long field trips, forgetting their original purpose in the excitement and losing a sense of distance from their object of study, with a consequent failure to reflect. The result of long stints of fieldwork can be an overdose of data, a loss of direction and subsequent delays in submitting your thesis. The advantages of staggering research trips are many. From initial visits to archives, initial interviews or participant observation, you can reassess and readjust your approach quite quickly to prepare for a second or even third trip. This is obviously linked to the availability of money, and it may not be feasible for you to carry out fieldwork, especially abroad, more than once. In this case your preparation must be even more thorough to reduce the chances of poor access to material or the discovery that there is inadequate material to collect.

Categorising data

Once you have collected your data, the process of analysis begins. This process is, of course, very much dependent on the type of data you have. However, no matter what the data, you do need some kind of system to categorise, compartmentalise and store it ready for easy access. An outline of your research project, broken down into provisional chapters, will be enormously useful when you are sifting through and analysing stacks of documents, interview transcripts and other sources collected from fieldwork. Simply place all relevant information for, say, chapter 1, in a box or pile. By marking all the piles or boxes with the relevant chapter numbers, you can begin to work on a chapter at a time without having to wade through all the documents, transcripts, etc. Unfortunately, this neat division of sources is not possible with such things as interview transcripts or notes in which you have asked several different questions pertaining to various parts of the thesis. The trick here is to read through the notes or transcripts with an array of different coloured pens. Mark specific passages, quotes or sections with a colour that represent a particular chapter. Another method of organising is to use themed index cards, on the same principle as the coloured pen example. Other, more up-to-date methods of sorting and categorising your data include the use of specially designed software packages which aid the process of organising and coding your data.

A crucial part of the secret of success in completing such a large piece of work is structure and order. And, although you should bear in mind your research questions and hypotheses whilst analysing data, you must remain adaptable, otherwise you may miss an opportunity to discover new or different patterns of information not accounted for in your desk-bound calculations. You need to revisit your research questions in the light of the analysis of the material gathered.

Stages of the research process

The final section of this chapter has two important aims: first, to recap on the different steps of research that we have discussed thus far by visu-alising them in a boxes-and-arrows flow chart. The purpose here is to understand how the various research steps that have been introduced relate to one another and to give an overview of the process by which the end destination of data-collection is reached. The second aim is to discuss how the research process can be cut up into stages. Although it may be argued that this is an artificial approach, given the *reflexive* nature of research, you will find that it is essential to have signposts to assist you during the three years of study. Signposts and stages are all intended to give order to a process that would be otherwise difficult to see as a whole. The model of the research process offered here is only *one* way (of many) of doing things: the important point is that everyone needs a model or plan of the research process, however artificial this may seem.

The story so far

Figure 3 aims to give an overview of all the areas of research that have been discussed in this and previous chapters. It also shows the interconnectedness of the various steps. The arrows indicate the direction of progression from box 1 to box 12.

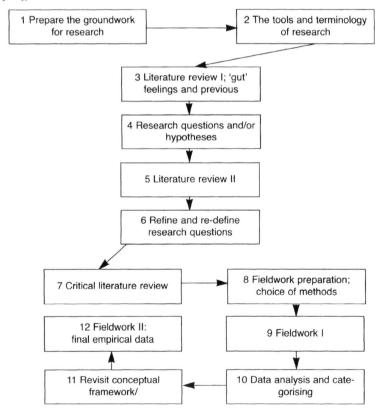

Figure 3: Steps of the research process

Spending time considering and planning out the first two steps of the doctoral process, represented by boxes 1 and 2, is essential in order to carry out the subsequent stages to maximum effect. Boxes 1 and 2 represent what I described in chapters 1 and 2, that is, familiarising yourself with the nature of doctoral research, the mechanics of the process and the tools needed to undertake it. Once you know what you are talking about, and no longer need to stop every five minutes to look up the meaning of 'ontological', you can get started on the various steps of the literature review on and around your topic (box 3).

As we have seen, this first encounter with the literature should confirm existing hunches or inform you (broadly) of the specific area and questions you wish to explore. By returning to the literature once the research questions or hypotheses have been refined and defined more sharply (box 6), you can begin to structure and focus your further reading more clearly. This is essential, because the number and length of books, articles, texts and texts on texts can be simply overwhelming. You are now ready for the critical literature review (box 7), after which your topic area, question(s) and methodological approach should be quite clear. You should be also now in a position to think about *how* you are going to answer the questions you have developed. This means deciding on the *type, unit* and *level* of analysis. The next step is to choose which *method(s)* to employ and which *data* to collect for your study. Thus, very thorough preparations are needed for fieldwork (box 8), in which the necessary data to answer your research questions or validate and refute your hypotheses will be collected (box 9). Boxes 10 to 12 represent work that will be undertaken in the final stage of research, sometimes called the post-empirical stage. It is clear that original hypotheses and theoretical approaches need to be revisited whilst analysing and categorising the data, as these will, to a certain extent, have been guiding the choice of data in the first place. Box 12 represents the final possibility of adding or filling any gaps in the project's empirical research. This is not as dramatic as it sounds, because at this point it may only mean getting your hands on a specific document, speech or last-minute interview.

The purpose of figure 3 is to visualise the steps that the previous chapters have discussed in more detail. By doing this, you can begin to see how they are all interwoven and bound by a certain *logic*. It is important to grasp 'the essentials and logic' of research (Punch, 2000a, 7) before starting a large project: the diagram emphasises how the literature review(s), research questions, hypotheses, and choice of methods used in a piece of research are inextricably linked. All of these components make up the research 'process', which should be seen as a 'series of linked activities moving from a beginning to an end' (Bouma and Atkinson, 1995, 9). However, as we have seen, this does not mean, for example, that the literature review is completed early on and never returned to at subsequent stages of the process.

The stages of doctoral research

Although the idea of stages of research may be somewhat artificial, in that they may not always follow the same sequence in every instance, there are certain elements of the research process that are common to all projects. Stages impose a kind of discipline on a complex business and many books on research offer models of various kinds. Figure 4, however, is specifically designed to give an overview of the doctoral process. Reflecting this process, the table is divided into three broad stages, representing the three years of a doctoral degree, and subdivided into several smaller stages. The balance of work within the three broader stages will very much depend on your discipline and topic, but also your strengths and weaknesses as an individual and your financial position. The model is for a full-time student wishing to finish a doctorate in three years. A part-time student could simply label the three stages years 1–2, 3–4 and 5–6 respectively. The point of this figure is not to repeat the information given above, but rather to add a temporal dimension to the idea of research stages and to add an 'action' column, in which extra information on other activities that doctoral students could – and should – be doing is included.

The first and most important thing to note is that this model of the doctoral research process is an oversimplification of a complex undertaking. (It is, after all, an abstraction based on my research, observation and personal experience). As I have pointed out, this book does not discuss the important theme of – and the table does not take into account – the psychological aspects of doing research, which can undoubtedly impinge on your ability to organise, structure and prioritise your work. Second, the stages of research are not divided and separate as in this artificial example, instead a continuous process of *reflexivity* takes place throughout the whole period of study. You need to constantly refer back to your research questions or hypotheses, whilst analysing data or reviewing literature, to help you sort the wood from the trees – otherwise you could end up reading everything on a given topic – and so that you do not lose sight of what it is you are trying to research.

The 'action' column suggests activities that could, as far as possible, accompany and facilitate the logic of the research project. For example,

Stage I	Sequence of research stages	Action
	1. Formulate your research problem; articulate your 'hunch' or tentative proposition	Learn tools and terminology of research; initial exploratory literature review
	2. Re-define and focus your topic and proposition; 3. Select your variables or means of 'testing' your questions 4. Have clear central research questions or key hypotheses	Second literature review. In addition, seek support by bouncing ideas off peers/friends/supervisor and by attending conferences for networking; undertake critical literature review
	5. Locate approach vis-à-vis others: begin writing the first chapter, setting out stages 1-4; 6. Select methods of enquiry 7. Produce a chapter outline of the whole thesis	Clarify your methodological approach Be familiar with debates/schools of thought/methods used and approaches on chosen topic; apply for external funding for fieldwork
Stage II	8. Prepare ground for fieldwork	Locate data; contact archives, institutions, individuals, etc.
	9. Sketch out fieldwork plan	Give conference papers; possibly publish; seek external feedback on proposed topic
	10. Fieldwork	Data collection: interviews, archives, questionnaires etc.
Stage III	11. Data analysis	Categorise data ready for analysis; analyse data
	12. Evaluate data 13. Redefine central research questions or hypotheses in the light of empirical data analysis.	Possibly publish your preliminary results; analysis and interpretation of data; relate evidence to research questions asked, draw conclusions

Figure 4. Possible stages of the doctoral process

none of the reflection and analysis mentioned above takes place in a vacuum with you hunched over a pile of books: rather there is a need for exposure and exchange of ideas not only with your supervisor but also with your peers and friends. Presenting your ideas to colleagues in seminars and at conferences is an essential part of academic life, along with gaining teaching experience as a postgraduate and publication, all of which will help you to refine and define your own ideas. One method of refining a research agenda is to tell a non-specialist (your mum, perhaps) in lay terms what it is exactly that you are studying or analysing. If you can sum up your topic and research questions crisply in a few sentences after having undertaken a thorough, and critical, review of the literature, you are ready to gather the evidence for your doctorate.

Stage I

By the end of stage I (year 1) you should have underpinned your hunch or hypothesis with a detailed literature review and have already decided on an approach to adopt, including which methods and sources to use. In addition, you ought now to be in a position to apply to external funding bodies for fieldwork expenses, a process that will take a long time to prepare, wait for an answer and deliver any payments. For this reason, you must start thinking about it at the earliest opportunity. Equally, this is the time to go over everything you have done so far and put it into written form, for although stage 14 suggests such a concept as a 'writing-up' stage, this is in fact a continual process and should certainly not be left to the very end. Like a runner who continually trains but refuses to race, you will never reach your goal if you put off the job of actually writing. And as a runner has to do a variety of different training sessions, from long-distance runs through to short, sharp, repetitions, in order to prepare for race-day, so your doctoral student's race-day also requires a variety of training regimes. Therefore, you need to write conference papers, notes and articles and draft and re-draft your thesis to prepare for the production of a very long text. The process of reflection includes constant feedback from supervisors, peers and friends on *written work* at every stage of the research process, thus preventing you from 'going off at a tangent', something to be wary of when planning long stints of fieldwork away from your institution.

Stage II

This is around the time you should be thinking about upgrading to a PhD. This depends, of course, on your home institutional regulations, although many doctoral students are usually registered for an MPhil in the first instance, unless they already have an MA and have already undertaken substantial research training. This is also the time to think about presenting papers at conferences in order to receive external feedback from the wider academic community *before* embarking on fieldwork. The feedback process will assist you in compiling your fieldwork plan, or your 'map', which will remind you of your questions, *where* you need to go to find the data and *what* data to collect. The bulk of the data collection is ideally done in the second year, thus leaving the third year free for analysing and writing up the data. If you categorise your data clearly and, if possible, according to the chapters of your thesis, the task of analysing it and 'meshing' it with your (theoretical) approach will be much easier. After an initial analysis of empirical data, it may be possible to publish a paper using your literature review (and indicating any 'gaps' found) and adding a little of the empirical data collected. It would not be wise to produce a huge paper on all of the major findings in the thesis, as this would make the book of the doctorate less attractive both to publishers and those likely to purchase it.

Stage III
Stage III is dominated by the reflexivity mentioned earlier, for data collected needs to be analysed and interpreted with an eye to the central research questions or key hypotheses developed throughout the research and with an eye to *new* questions and avenues of enquiry that may open up. Again, it is a good idea to try to 'write-up' during the period of analysis of data. Once the data analysis is finished, you should be able to enjoy editing the entire text. If you drop your thesis of, say, eight loose chapters on the floor, gather it up in a random order of chapter numbers, and find that it reads as well as before, something has gone radically wrong with its logic and structure. It is a good idea to have the thesis soft-bound at an early draft stage – and bear in mind this is only a draft – and read it from page 1 to the end to see if the constituent parts of your work actually join and flow together. It is interesting to witness how previously smooth-reading, self-contained chapters or sections suddenly crunch and grind against each other once bound and read together. Having the text soft-bound eases the task of smoothing out any abrupt changes in style or content and ensuring a common thread runs throughout the work. If you have been careful with referencing and bibliographical details, editing the whole thesis chapter by chapter can be a pleasurable experience. Your aim is to have one 'voice' running through the entire thesis, for your writing style will probably have changed as you progressed and learned how to sum up arguments succinctly.

Summary

Among the points covered in chapter 4 has been: the introduction of some popular research methods used in doctoral studies to obtain empirical data (I deliberately did not include technical statistical packages, as these require much more than a brief overview and you must consult an appropriate textbook), the notion of triangulation, fieldwork preparation and the stages of the doctoral process. The key points can be summed up thus:

* Methods should be chosen for their appropriateness in answering the questions posed (remember the 'question–method' match).
* Most of the methods discussed briefly above can be used in quantitative *and* qualitative research strategies.
* Try not to employ just *one* method of data collection, but attempt to mix methods and data to add to your project's validity (often called 'triangulation' of methods or data).
* Prepare thoroughly for fieldwork, long *before* actually leaving. Contact individuals, organisations, institutions and arrange meetings and archival visits, etc.
* Consider the *logic* of the different components that make up the doctoral process and how these link with one another.
* Think of the doctoral process as a set of stages. Dividing up the process can add order and transparency to your research, whilst allowing you to set yourself targets at specific moments during your studies.

Further reading:

Bell, J. (1993) *Doing Your Research Project. A Guide to First-Time Researchers in Education and Social Science,* Buckingham, Open University Press.

Bryman, A. (2001) *Social Research Methods,* Oxford, Oxford University Press.

Grant, W., (2000) 'Elite Interviewing: A Practical Guide', Institute for German Studies Discussion Paper, No. 11.

Kumar, R. (1999) *Research Methodology. A Step-By-Step Guide for Beginners,* London/Thousand Oaks/New Delhi, Sage.

Neuman, W. L. (2000) *Social Research Methods. Qualitative and Quantitative Approaches,* Boston, Allyn & Bacon, 4th edition.

Peters, G. B. (1998) *Comparative Politics. Theory and Methods,* Basingstoke, Macmillan.

Punch, K. F. (2000a) *Introduction to Social Research. Quantitative and Qualitative Approaches,* London/Thousand Oaks/New Delhi, Sage.

Silverman, D. (2000) *Doing Qualitative Research. A Practical Handbook,* London/Thousand Oaks/New Delhi, Sage.

5 Supervision, the viva and other matters of importance

Introduction

This chapter covers a number of the most important factors in doctoral studies:

- a guide to the student–supervisor relationship and how you can get the most from it
- an in-depth exposition of the viva
- advice on writing your thesis and getting published
- a discussion on ethics and plagiarism in research
- advice on how to use postgraduate training
- a discussion on the utility of a PhD.

First, I begin with a look at the nature of the student–supervisor relationship, as this is one of the most important components of any successful postgraduate research project. Although practices are very diverse, this chapter presents core characteristics that need to be borne in mind by the student before and during the supervision process. The emphasis here is on the proactive role you should play to ensure you get the most out of this relationship.

The viva, possibly the single most important event in a postgraduate's academic life, is an event about which little is published. The manner in which it is carried out differs greatly from university to university, but, again, some core features can be teased out to help you prepare in advance. It may well be the most important examination of your life, and it is the one for which you can exert the most influence over the agenda. The mystery surrounding this event adds to students' woes and thickens considerably the general mystery surrounding the doctoral process.

After some advice on how to write a long piece of research, which, contrary to common belief, is not best done in a flurry of activity in the last months of your registration period, the following section offers some tips on publishing. The focus here is on academic journals and your thesis, once it has been accepted. It has become increasingly important for those wishing to pursue an academic career to have a PhD *and* to have published something.

The succeeding section sets out the ways you can gain the most from research training, seminars, conferences and workshops. It begins by explaining the differences between the last three and then goes on to highlight the benefits they can have on your research. Included in this chapter is a section on ethics and plagiarism in research, topics that, since the explosion of the use of the Web, have gained dramatically in relevance. All researchers, need to be aware of how their research affects the people they are researching, and they need to consider the origins of their sources and how they cite and disseminate their findings.

The final section deals with the utility of a doctorate, which is discussed with reference to the skills necessary to complete one. These transferable and employment-related skills that are learnt or enhanced by the process of research are, often, sought by prospective employers.

Supervisors and supervisions

The student–supervisor relationship is perhaps *the* crucial component of the postgraduate research process: certainly it is comparable in importance to mastering the tools and terminology. It is also one of the most difficult aspects to give good, solid advice on, as students and supervisors are individuals, and vary greatly in their opinions, attitudes, preferences, expectations and ways of doing things. For example, one particular student may feel the need for constant feedback, whilst the supervisor with whom they have been paired prefers the 'light-touch' approach, that is, they wish to have infrequent meetings and they place a great deal of emphasis on student independence (see Phillips and Pugh, 1994, 10). There is an obvious danger of a mismatch of expectations here, which is bound to lead to problems. Equally, the appointed supervisor may have a completely different world-view to you, which could make for interesting debates, but could also end up with you covering topics of the supervisor's choice rather than your own.

Supervisory skills are of both a professional and a personal nature. A good supervisor not only needs to know what constitutes a professional piece of research, including being familiar with the 'nuts and bolts' of the process discussed in this book, but they also need to have certain interpersonal skills to be able to offer advice and a listening ear to matters that go beyond the thesis. You will usually have some influence in the choice of supervisor in the first place, although this depends very much on your funding situation. If you are a fee-paying student who wishes to be supervised by Professor X, then you may well get your way, providing your work is in the professor's area, he or she is willing to take you on, and he or she does not already have too many doctoral students (the usual limit is around six full-time students per supervisor). Check university prospectuses and look up the respective department's Website for information on individual scholars. If you are applying for external postgraduate funding, it is likely that the department through which you apply will allocate you the most relevant supervisor, as the match between the student's topic and the prospective supervisor is a criterion in assessing applications. Remember, as I mentioned in chapter 1, it is by no means essential or indeed desirable to have as a supervisor a first-ranking authority on your precise subject. However, it is crucial that your supervisor is conversant with what level and volume of work constitutes an MPhil or PhD. You need to understand the fundamentals of the research process, discussed in the previous chapters, before you begin your research. If your supervisor does not ensure that you have the requisite knowledge and skills to undertake your work, make sure you do it yourself. Both the skills you bring with you and the supervisor's academic experience are key factors affecting the overall dynamics of the student–supervisor relationship (Brown and Atkins, 1993, 118).

One positive thing about the student–supervisor relationship is that both parties have a vested interest in the success of the project. You, the student, usually want to finish within the period of funding, or, if you are self-funding, as quickly as possible. Supervisors' success or failure in helping students to complete their work within a reasonable time will be used, in part, as a measure of their own competence by their peers.

Although supervisors and supervisions are very heterogeneous, there are a number of broad points to be aware of, which will facilitate the student–supervisor relationship and assist you in gaining the most from it.

Stages of the supervision process

The process can be broken down into broad, overlapping stages. You will begin with initial, intense meetings, then there will be the main, everyday experience of supervision, through the fieldwork period and, finally, you can expect to reach a point where you are practically autonomous and need only infrequent exchanges with your supervisor. The following sets out some of the things to remember at the relevant stages of the supervision process:

Initial period

The first thing to remember is that a supervisor is not a higher deity. You cannot and should not expect your supervisor to do everything for you, spot gaps in the literature or come up with interesting projects for you. What they can do is to help you achieve all of this. In order to get the most out of a supervisor and the supervision meeting, take a proactive role, establishing early on a pattern of working, including the regularity of meetings and the format supervision meetings will take. If appropriate, you can discuss the type of guidance or feedback that you find most helpful. Do not be afraid to ask about the supervisor's availability and accessibility, especially during term-time when they probably have to teach. Where possible give the supervisor something to read prior to supervisions – this could be chapter outlines, ideas for general research questions or actual text. Make a list of the themes or topics you wish to discuss in the supervision and let the supervisor have this with the work, so that the supervision has a structure, instead of just sitting around chatting about very interesting matters for an hour.

Main period

Always engage with the supervisor's advice, whether you like it or not, as there is nothing more frustrating for a supervisor than spending hours poring over a text and making suggestions only to find out that not a single remark has been tackled, refuted or taken on board. Also, do not make the mistake of waiting and holding on to a piece of work until it is 'perfect' or 'finished' before showing your supervisor, as this is a recipe for not finishing the thesis on time. On the other hand, avoid handing in shoddy work, that has not even been checked for spelling, as the supervisor will spend hours trying to wade through grammatical and typographical mistakes, without actually being able to concentrate on the substance. Show your work to colleagues and peers beforehand, actively discussing problems with them. Remember, the supervisor is not there to rewrite your thesis (as this is both unreasonable and dishonest). If you are a non-native speaker, try to have someone check through your language prior to handing it in. If you present your supervisor with a well-written text, he or she is more likely to be able to give you careful, clear feedback. There are different types of supervisors, of course, ranging from those who supply you with minute detailed comments, to broad-brush types who look to the wider picture, seeing whether your work contains good ideas and fits with the relevant literature. In an ideal world your supervisor(s) will be able to play both roles, depending on your work's needs.

To ensure a good relationship, stick to your side of the student–supervisor bargain by keeping to schedules you have jointly set, arriving on time for supervisions and not pestering your supervisor at every available opportunity (Lawton, 1999, 9). Supervisors are usually very busy academics who are under immense pressure to publish, teach and, increasingly, to administer like seasoned managers. Thus, supervisions, viewed from the supervisors' perspective, are further claims on the diminishing research time they have at their disposal. By preparing for supervisions as I have suggested above, you facilitate the supervision experience and maximise the time spent discussing *your* work, rather than a grammatical mistake or something tangential to your thesis. Finally, take a record of the supervision, noting the topics discussed, the supervisor's comments and the work to be undertaken before the next meeting. Some departments will have a special supervision form for this purpose. Run through these points with your supervisor at the end of the meeting, not least to ensure that you are both clear on what has been discussed.

Fieldwork period
This may well be the period of time in which you will see your supervisor least. However, with the help of email and telephone it is easy to remain in touch. Usually, if you are spending a relatively long period away from your university, you will be affiliated to an appropriate institution and you will possibly have a temporary supervisor allocated to you and your project. A good fieldwork plan, worked out in advance with, and sanctioned by, your supervisor, will act as a 'map' with which you can gauge your progress. It should also include stages at which you ought to contact, or send work to, your supervisor, in order to prevent you drifting off your intended course. If possible, you should continue to send written work to your supervisor during this period, as this helps you avoid isolation and keeps your supervisor informed of your progress.

The final period
By the closing stages of your doctorate there is no doubt that you should know more about the *empirical* content of your thesis than your supervisor. However, the supervisor still ought to know what constitutes a PhD, in particular knowing the quality and amount of data you require to be able

to submit your thesis with reasonable expectations of success. Technically, you have the final say on what actually goes into the thesis and when to submit it, but it would be foolish to do so against the explicit advice of your supervisor, unless of course you have no faith whatsoever in his or her judgement. In this case, seek someone else's opinion. If you have had plenty of interaction with colleagues and peers and you have presented your thoughts at conferences and workshops, you should be able to assess whether your supervisor is right or not. The converse situation may also occur: it may be that your supervisor wants you to submit your thesis, although you personally feel that it is not ready. This scenario is likely to become more common in the future: first, as departments are under pressure for students to finish within specific time periods and, second, as many students treat their thesis like a painting, to which they are always wanting to add just one more brushstroke.

The frequency of meetings with your supervisor during the writing-up stage will very much depend on the individual. If you have maintained a continuous process of writing, which you should have, then your supervisor will have already read and re-read numerous drafts of your chapters and it will be left to you to join them up into a cohesive draft thesis. If, on the other hand, you have saved yourself for the writing-up period, then you will certainly need considerable guidance during this phase.

Supervision training and joint supervisions

It is generally recognised that there is a fundamental lack of training provision for prospective supervisors. To become a supervisor, an academic must, at the very least, spend some time in the company of a more experienced colleague in the position of co-supervisor. More recently, there have been suggestions for the introduction of a formal training process for supervisors, which will no doubt be resisted by the more conservative members of the academic community. The ESRC in the UK has been at the forefront of opinion calling for institutions to have 'formal systems in place for monitoring the performance of supervisors, for identifying the training and development needs of supervisors and for ensuring that these are met' (ESRC, 2001, 11). The fact that there is no formal supervision training scheme means that supervisors' styles vary considerably. This is why it is essential that you attempt to structure your supervision sessions as I have suggested above.

Joint supervisions are becoming increasingly popular throughout departments in the UK, not least because this is also strongly recommended by funding bodies. There are, of course, both advantages and disadvantages to joint supervision, although I would suggest that the former far outweigh the latter. The advantages are obvious: you have two academic minds poring over your work, twice the chance of someone spotting mistakes or adding useful information and twice the number of contacts and networks that the supervisors bring with them. For this to work effectively, one supervisor *must* be designated as the principal supervisor and each should be allocated specific tasks, for example, supervisor 1 could focus on the methodology and supervisor 2 could have overall responsibility for the empirical content of the thesis. Regardless of the division of labour between supervisors, it is essential that you and they are clear exactly what it is *before* you begin your studies. It is essential to meet both supervisors at the beginning of the initial period and to establish the modus operandi for the duration of your research.

On the negative side, joint supervision could lead to you receiving competing and contradictory advice or ontological views, and a lack of a sense of continuity. Problems may arise if the supervisors do not share the same intellectual view or when the information flow within the triangle of supervisor 1–you–supervisor 2 is insufficient. To avoid such problems all three people must be kept abreast of everything that has been written, suggested or researched as a part of the project.

The viva

Seldom has there been so little written on a topic of such importance to so many nervous postgraduates. 'Viva' is the abbreviated form of viva voce, which literally means 'the living voice', or in a modern parlance, a jolly good discussion – if not a heated debate. For a doctoral student, it is the name given to the oral examination which marks the passage from student to professional academic – if, of course, you are successful. Mystery shrouds this finale because there is (a) no set way of going about it (b) because practices vary across institutions – and vary greatly across different countries – and (c) because there is so little information published on it. This section will, however, draw out some of the common features of the viva examination in the UK in order to give you an idea of what you can expect.

First, let's briefly discuss the nature of the viva itself, before giving a breakdown of what the actual viva examination could look like.

- The purpose of the viva is for the examiners to decide whether your thesis has reached the required standard for a PhD or not, and also to make sure the work they have received in written form is really your own.
- The viva in the UK appears a less intimidating affair in comparison to Sweden, Germany, the US and many other countries, where the candidate really does have to defend his or her thesis against an 'opponent', a large committee or in public (or all three). The rationale for the viva in the UK is really to test a candidate's knowledge and understanding of the material that they have presented in written form. Some people understand the viva as a *defence* of a piece of work. Whilst you will spend time justifying certain approaches or methods in your study, I think the term 'defence' conjures up an image of a candidate under attack, which I do not believe is a helpful way of understanding the viva. There is no reason why you should not positively *enjoy* the viva, given that this will probably be the only time that two people, in this case two experts, beyond family and friends, will, or should, enthusiastically engage with your work over a prolonged period. In order to go some way to ensuring you will enjoy the viva, learn all the key terms and terminology associated with the research process. With a full command of the terms, concepts and their roles in research introduced in this book, it is unlikely that you will be unsettled by a technical question. This is an important point, because, as I shall discuss below, many examiners focus on concepts, methods, methodology, approach and your theoretical framework, precisely because it is very difficult, if not impossible, for them to know more than you about the empirical data you have presented on your topic.
- Opinions differ as to how much knowledge the candidate should possess of subjects and themes peripheral to the thesis. If you have undertaken a thorough enough literature review and embedded your thesis in wide-ranging debates, this is unlikely to be a problem. However, if you find the examiners drifting off your topic with a question linked to a pet theme of their own, be sure to refer back to the objectives of your own thesis. It is a good idea to have in your own mind the key themes *you* would like to discuss in the viva.
- The precise point at which you submit your thesis is a decision best made together with your supervisor. However, before you do submit you should go over the whole body of work carefully and make sure your argument is coherent and consistent throughout; ensure you actually do analyse what you say you will in the introduction; be sure your methodology section is robust and you have discussed carefully

your approach, the cases you use, and so on. Also, bear in mind you will almost certainly need to justify your choice of research methods and methodological approach.

- Go into the viva with a positive attitude. In all your previous examinations the questions have been framed by someone else, this time *you* have chosen the terrain .

- In preparation for the exam, you should read your thesis through very carefully. Depending on what type of person you are, you can either make detailed notes or, what is probably more effective, list the central points your thesis makes. You need to get these central points across in the exam itself: What is the contribution of your thesis to scholarship? Why did you chose this case study? Why did you use this approach as opposed to the more orthodox approach? How would you do things differently if you had to start all over again? The last question is indicative of the sharp learning curve that postgraduate students climb during their studies – you should end up wiser than when you began, not least in the matter of spotting potential obstacles and dead-ends in research. Most of all, anticipate and visualise the viva, imagine in your mind's eye these types of questions and your answers. Be honest with yourself, identify the weak points of the thesis and try to think of probing questions you may have to deal with.

- It may be possible, time permitting, to have a 'mock viva' with academics in your department who have experience as internal and external examiners (Phillips and Pugh, 1994, 140). Do try and get someone to go over the whole text for you before you hand in the thesis, as you probably will no longer be able to see any punctuation mistakes after repeatedly re-reading the text. Devote most of your preparation time to answering questions on your key arguments (especially your theoretical arguments) *not* on factual details, because it is difficult to predict just which fact you will be tested on – the examiners will point you to a page number in the case of a query, in any case. How you actually revise for the exam will differ from individual to individual. Some choose to write copious notes and whittle them down gradually by committing the key arguments of the piece to memory. Others *know* the key arguments, the theoretical approach and the rationale behind choosing a particular case study, because they have been thinking about them for years. Whatever method you choose, you need to know your own thesis inside out.

- You should take a copy of your thesis and two pens with you into the viva. Some people use coloured Post-it notes to indicate particularly important sections. My advice would be not to refer to the thesis in front of you unless you are asked to clarify something specific. You should not take any notes you have used to revise with you into the examination.

The actors involved in, and the substance of, the viva

Who will be examining you in the viva?
The examination panel usually consists of an external and internal examiner, and possibly a chairperson (who does not need to be an expert in your field, but ought to be familiar with the university's regulations on vivas). Sometimes your supervisor may be allowed to sit in on proceedings (unless you wish otherwise), but he or she is not allowed to intervene in any way at all. You may, of course, request that your supervisor is *not* present.

Let us start with the chair. This person usually opens proceedings by introducing the external and internal examiners, then kicks off the viva with a gentle opening question, such as, 'what does your thesis contribute to the scholarly literature on German–Polish relations?' You can – and should – obviously rehearse the 'contribution to the literature' question at home. However, do not, in general, rehearse questions – in particular, avoid trotting out in response to one question something that has been rehearsed as an answer to another. If there is no chair, then the internal examiner will probably do the introductions.

The external examiner is usually chosen for his or her authority in your field and will be somebody who has had no involvement in the genesis of your thesis, including the reading of draft chapters or commenting on its central ideas.

The internal examiner is likely to be someone in your department, faculty or school who must not be your supervisor, but who works in an area close to the field under examination. Their job, generally speaking, is to examine the thesis but also to be supportive to the candidate. However, this is not always the case; it has been known for situations to arise in which one examiner attempts to impress the other. In such a scenario, simply concentrate on explaining your thesis.

You may have some input into who your external examiner is going to be, but a few words of warning are necessary. Do not run away with the idea that the biggest celebrity in your field would be the best person to examine your thesis. First, 'living legends' will probably not have the time; second, they may have a particular approach to your topic and may not be sympathetic to your 'innovative' approach; and third, you will be judged by the result of your viva and not by the standing or fame of your external examiner. It is far better to have passed your viva than to have failed with a very well known external. The two advantages of big-name examiners are that they can be useful when approaching publishers for the publication of your work, and they may stand out as referees on job applications. Finally, *do not* go overboard with citing a particular scholar or – as Phillips and Pugh suggest – actually citing a scholar once you have found out they are to be your external examiner. It is not necessary to make sure they feature heavily in your bibliography (Phillips and Pugh, 1994, 138); I agree with Peter Burnham that external examiners are unlikely to be impressed by such a move, especially if the works cited are not absolutely crucial to the key debates in the thesis (see Burnham, 1997, 194). On the other hand, you do need to check the external examiner's published work to be aware of the types of arguments that he or she has put forward before, and so anticipate and avoid inadvertent collisions which might result in the examiner's work becoming the focus of the viva.

How does the viva procedure work?

Once you submit your thesis to the university, it is their responsibility to send it off to both the external and internal examiners. You have to wait approximately two to three months before the actual viva takes place. Each examiner writes a separate report on the thesis in accordance with your university's guidelines, and they then exchange reports and discuss their views on the day of the viva. Good examiners will then discuss the format of the viva and how the questioning is to be divided up, thus giving structure to the proceedings. In the viva itself, which usually takes from one and a half to a maximum of three hours, the external examiner takes the lead. The final say on whether you pass, fail, resubmit or otherwise rests with the external examiner, not the internal examiner or the chair.

What are the examiners examining in the viva?

The first thing you must do is check your university regulations, as these may differ slightly from the advice offered here. Your thesis will need to be a certain length – usually between 70, 000 and 80, 000 words excluding footnotes and bibliography – and the examiners can 'refer' your work, that is, ask you to revise and re-submit it, if it is clearly over your university's limit. Your thesis must also conform to certain presentational, formatting and referencing conventions, again stipulated in your university's regulations, often available in the main library.

A more serious factor examiners will be looking for is the engagement of your work with the relevant literature in your field. If you have carried out a thorough and critical literature review this will not be a problem, provided you have chosen the most relevant literature. Another question may focus on the area or period you have chosen in your study. Going back to our German–Polish example, an examiner may argue that a longer period of analysis would have been more appropriate. Or he or she may argue that another country should have been included in the study to give it wider relevance. For this reason, when preparing for the viva, go over all of these types of questions in your mind.

A particular area of focus will be your methodology. Many of the debates touched on above will be especially relevant here, for example, those around the use of qualitative and quantitative research, the issue of bias in your sources, the notion of triangulation, the relevance of your (theoretical) approach to the empirical section of the thesis and your awareness of the ontological and epistemological assumptions of the approach you have adopted. As I have hinted above, examiners tend to head straight for this section, because it is crucial to the understanding of the thesis and your initiation into the profession. The examiners should also know less about the empirical work than you, otherwise your work would not be deemed to be sufficiently original. You need to strike a balance between being able to justify the components of your methodology and becoming defensive. The latter can lead to you 'clamming up' or feeling offended. Expect such abrupt statements as 'I have major reservations about the limitations of your empirical data.' Again, just as in the process of research itself, do not get upset, but reflect on what is being said before answering. Carefully go over the rationale behind the choice of methods and sources and *why* you believe the data not to be limited. If you have done your homework, and you know all the arguments likely to be deployed against your use of, say, a single case-study method, then you will be in a position to discuss the examiner's reservations.

You need to prepare a solid argument regarding the original research in your thesis, as this will be another area the examiners are very likely to focus on, given that it is the largest element of the requirements for achieving a PhD. Your university's regulations will speak of a thesis needing to make a 'substantial contribution to knowledge' which, in plain English, means that you must have produced original research on a given topic and embedded it firmly in the 'received wisdom' of a particular field (i.e. new data or a new interpretation of an established assumption. See Silverman, 2000, chapter 4, for a full exploration of 'originality' in research.) You should also have presented a structured and logical argument in which this new material is integrated. If you have managed to fulfil the above, it is very likely that the examiners will recommend certain parts or all of the thesis for publication.

I would like to reiterate a few things regarding questioning in the viva:

- do not become defensive, but try to reflect on the questions that are put to you, regardless of the manner in which they are expressed. The examiners will be more impressed with someone who can take on board criticism or suggestions than with someone who is adamant that his or her approach is unimpeachable. You need to get the balance right on what you can and cannot afford to concede in a viva. Obviously, with questions concerning the originality of the thesis and its contribution to knowledge you ought not concede too much, given that these are crucial to actually gaining a PhD. Conceding on areas where you might have done something differently and *even better* than you actually did is probably safe, provided that you are confident that your thesis, as it stands, is good enough to pass.
- listen very carefully to the examiners' questions, and always ask for a question to be repeated if you do not fully understand it. Be very sure of the definitions of the concepts used in your work and be prepared to debate them.
- at all costs avoid going off into a long soliloquy which has little or nothing to do with the original question asked.

What are the different outcomes of the viva?
Basically, there are six types of outcome of the viva examination, three of which you can live with, three of which are to be avoided.

1. The thesis is passed outright with no corrections or modifications needed. This is extremely rare and depends on a number of things: first and most obvious, the quality of the thesis; and second, the examiners themselves. They may overlook a few typographical errors just to finish the process or because they think the thesis is wonderful.
2. The thesis is passed, but you are required to make minor revisions. The revisions are often of a presentational nature or involve correcting errors, for example, in dates, places, names, footnotes or bibliographical data. Usually you can expect to have the changes finished within a few weeks. The revisions are checked by the internal examiner only.
3. The thesis is passed subject to major revisions. In this case you need to resubmit the thesis within an agreed period of time, having revised the text according to the examiners' suggestions. This seems to be on the increase, as students are under enormous pressure to finish with three

years. If this happens, make sure you get *very* specific details of the changes required, so you can have a 'map' to work with. Both the external and the internal usually need to check that you have made the revisions necessary to obtain a doctorate.

4. The thesis is referred. This means that you need to substantially revise and re-submit the work, usually within one year from the viva, taking on board the criticisms of the examiners. You will have to attend another viva to satisfy the examiners.

5. The thesis is deemed of insufficient quality to warrant a PhD and an MPhil or MA is offered in its place. This is obviously to be avoided! The difference between an MPhil and PhD is the extent of original research in the thesis and its impact on, and integration with, existing scholarly literature. Check your university regulations for a precise definition of the differences between the two.

6. The thesis fails. This is a very rare scenario and there are procedures whereby a student may appeal against this, or any other, judgement.

After the viva you will be asked to leave the room for about ten to twenty minutes, while the examiners decide on the result – provided that they have not informed you of the outcome at the beginning (although if you are not told anything, this should not be taken as a negative sign) – and draft their joint report, setting out one of the options from the six above. As soon as you have passed your viva, after revisions or not, it is usual practice to begin using the title 'Dr' straight away, although officially, you have to wait until your degree is conferred at the appropriate ceremony. In the vast majority of cases you can look forward to enjoying a meal or a drink with the examiners shortly after the examination.

The process of writing a thesis

The following section is intended as a quick guide to the writing of your thesis. I have included a selection of literature at the end of this chapter which deals in far greater detail with such topics as style, grammar and punctuation. Here I outline some of the most salient aspects of any writing-up strategy.

There are several different types of 'writing' in a thesis. Amongst the most important are:

- writing notes
- drafting chapters
- writing conference/workshop/seminar papers
- writing your thesis
- the so-called 'writing-up' stage.

While the above can be treated as distinct from one another – in varying degrees – they all have one purpose, and that is to contribute to the production of your thesis. Clearly, taking notes is not the same as putting the finishing touches to your final thesis. However, you can go some way towards closing the gap between the two by writing notes that can *easily* be transformed into prose. If notes are patchy, written in code or illegible, they will not lend themselves to a quick translation into text. One efficient way of taking notes, be it of a book you are reading or in an archive, is to enter them directly into a computer. This naturally raises the question of access to resources like laptop computers. If at all possible, get regular access to one, even if borrowed or shared with fellow researchers, as it does save an inordinate amount of time, and the results are at least legible and easily transferrable to your department or home computer to be integrated into your thesis.

Drafting and redrafting

Writing drafts of your work is an essential part of constructing a thesis. Throughout the research process your style and ability to write should develop and improve, so that by year three your very first chapter draft written somewhere in the first term will probably be unrecognisable as your own work. In order to improve, however, you must write. The best possible way of developing both your writing skills and your thesis quickly is to get your ideas down on paper and *give* the chapter/piece to peers and your supervisor(s). The process of creating a thesis is achieved via the interaction of ideas, not by sitting on your work until it is 'perfect'. The more feedback and constructive criticism you receive, the faster you will improve. Before giving anything to your supervisor check through it carefully, edit the text and, if possible, give it to a peer or friend to read through. It is not necessary for them to have an intimate knowledge of your topic, the point is to see if you are expressing yourself in a clear and coherent manner. The 'write–read–rewrite–read–give to a friend strategy' will ensure that your work reaches your supervisor in a clear, legible state, which, in turn, will ensure that your supervisor can give maximum attention to the subject matter and not have to concentrate on poor expression, grammatical mistakes and spelling errors.

The reflexive nature of research, and in particular the writing process, is captured by Blaxter *et al.*, when they suggest:

> Writing up your research should start early and become a regular and continuing activity. It is also likely to be an iterative or *cyclical* process [my emphasis]. That is, you will draft a section or chapter, then move on to some other activity, and return one or more times to redraft your original version. This is partly because as the totality of the research thesis or report takes shape, what you have written in subsequent sections affects what you wrote earlier and necessitates changes in it. (1997, 208–9)

It is important to be sensible and selective in your choice of reader-cum-critic. To the non-scholar, or 'civilian', academic writing seems strange, difficult, inaccessible and unappealing. To make matters worse, very few people you ask for advice will own up to having nothing useful to say, so an indiscriminate approach to the seeking of readers' advice will certainly result in a steady drizzle of questionable, well-intentioned advice, and may even provoke a storm of positively damaging criticism. Bear in mind that most people's notion of high-level writing is a 500-word article in a broadsheet newspaper or a journal like *The Economist*, or else an undergraduate textbook. These are not necessarily appropriate guides or models for academic prose.

Papers

Writing a conference or seminar paper is a different task altogether, as the subject is usually self-contained and usually shorter than a thesis chapter. Whereas the latter must connect with both the previous and subsequent chapters, a conference/seminar paper can stand alone. However, you want to be able to 'recycle' as much of the paper for your thesis as possible.

The task of writing such a paper is very good practice for an inexperienced researcher, as it forces you to deliver a 'tight', less wordy argument than is the case in many a thesis. You can use this experience to revisit your work with the intention of cutting out too much repetition – although some is necessary – sharpening the definitions of the concepts you use, and tightening your argument. The main thing is to make sure you gear any conference or seminar papers towards your topic or approach.

Writing strategies

The writing strategy you adopt may be driven by personal preferences or previous experience. Just as there is no single viva examination, there is no single successful writing strategy for a thesis. There are, however, two very big things you should not do:

- do not conceive of the writing-up phase as separate from the research process in general
- do not make the mistake of hanging on to work – however rough – for too long.

The first thing to note is that writing is a continuous process that ought to begin the minute you start your registration. Better still, you can begin beforehand. For an MA, MPhil or PhD you will need to draw up a research proposal. This usually marks the beginning of a thesis or dissertation.

A literature review is a very good way of starting to write a thesis. As you need to read the literature before you start, in any case, and also need to embed your own approach or find a novel one, there is no better place to start than this. Bearing in mind the advice given in chapter 3 – not merely to draw up an annotated bibliography – you should begin as soon as possible to record the relevant arguments, debates and texts on and around your subject. A literature review will eventually become an important section of your thesis. If you can construct your review according to appropriate, broad categories, you should be able to add works/arguments as you come across them without having to rewrite the whole review.

Always bear in mind the audience or readership of your work. Yes, you are writing it for your supervisor, but, beyond that, you need to imagine a reader who is not an absolute expert; for such an audience the frequent use of terms or concepts without explanation is plainly bad practice. Choose clear and concise phrases, sentences, paragraphs and style, as opposed to complex and multi-claused prose, and do not be afraid to repeat yourself in the text. You need to strike a balance between boring repetition which adds nothing to your argument and, for example, recurring observations that help contextualise and connect your empirical work with your conceptual framework. Remember, the idea is to help people follow a well-set-out, clearly expressed argument, not to dazzle or confuse with esoteric jargon. The latter is a hackneyed ploy adopted by some authors to disguise the fact that they have little of value to say.

Always remember that a thesis is a specialised scholarly work. There is not much room for flippancy or other varieties of wit: the world will judge your personality using other measures than the lightness of your authorial touch in this most specialised of literary forms. Aim to master the *academic* idiom. To get a feel of the variety of styles that people use in dissertations and theses, take a look at other students' end-products in the main library.

Some students find it very difficult to get to grips with the wealth of empirical material they gather from their fieldwork. You need to try and keep on top of your empirical material as you go along, otherwise you could 'drown' in it. If you do find yourself staring at sacks of collected material and unable to get started, one strategy is to write four or five chapters in telegraphic style, each chapter no longer than, say, ten pages, listing the main arguments presented and the sources you have used. In this way you can go over and over the respective sections or chapters while engaging with the empirical material you have gathered. Remember, whatever data you use ensure your references are in order from day one (see chapter 1 and appendix 2 for more on referencing), as improper referencing can lead to serious delays and accusations of plagiarism (see below).

Structure

When writing a long piece of research, pay particular attention to structure. If you present examiners with a long, rambling, illogical piece of work, you will fail, even if your thesis contains wonderful empirical revelations. If your empirical data do not relate to clear, precise questions or hypotheses, it will be difficult to know just what your contribution to research is. The best method of developing a robust structure to your thesis and argument is to draw up a thesis plan, setting out the headings of each chapter and subheadings within them. These will undoubtedly change or be moved around with time, but the point is to draw up and set out a 'map' for the writing process (see Delamont *et al.*, 1999, 119–20, for a good example of this). You should include dates by which you want to have finished certain sections, the titles of these sections and the amount of words given over to each, a necessary action given the word restrictions of a modern PhD thesis (most commonly about 80, 000 words).

You should begin each chapter with a succinct summary of the arguments contained therein. This forces you to cut your arguments to the bone and helps you assess whether your arguments are clear and logical. You will probably find that in the final version these summaries will be written last, but to begin with they serve as a way of structuring your thesis (see van Evera, 1997, 107). Ensure that you have enough 'signposts' in your chapters, indicating the 'direction your argument or discussion is taking' (Fairbairn and Winch, 2000, 77), but especially at the end of the chapters. It is useful to point out to the reader the obvious link between one chapter and the next.

A simple but hugely effective way to structure your writing is by setting up folders for each of your chapters. In each folder, collect relevant material for the chapter, and, having analysed the material and marked specific passages or sections, sit down and set about transferring the information from the folders into the sections and subsections of your thesis plan. At this stage the idea is simply to transfer the information and not to necessarily write beautiful prose. There are certain psychological gains to be had by seeing the material collected for each chapter decrease. Once you have added all the information for a specific section or even chapter, you can start the enjoyable process of 'write–read–edit–rewrite–re-read–edit'. Each time you go through this cycle, you end up with a slightly better product. After further amendment in response to selected peers and finally your supervisor(s), this section or chapter can be put to one side.

Publication: working papers, journals and books

As with most of the sections in this chapter, the following can only offer some pointers to a process that differs widely across disciplinary boundaries. My intention is to focus on some broad and fundamental points that will be relevant to most social science subject areas.

Working papers and journals

The first thing to do is to check whether your department or centre has a working paper series, as this offers an ideal outlet for first-time publications. Working papers can be distributed widely and provoke valuable feedback from friends, family, peers and academics. This is particularly the case if the series is also available for downloading on your department's Website. A working paper can be seen as a step on the road to a journal article: after getting feedback and refining and defining your terms and concepts you will have a far better article than when you started.

Seek advice from your supervisor or other members of staff in your department on which journal to go to with your revised and updated working paper. Some journals have a particularly long lead-time between submission and publication, in some cases years – obviously an undesirable prospect for a doctoral student. A better idea is to look for a specialist journal – and not necessarily the most high in prestige – in your area of study, as they are more likely to publish something from a doctoral student which directly relates to a particular specialism. It is common, and perfectly acceptable, to publish your work in an article co-written with other, more senior colleagues. In fact it is usually better to be the second-named author of a good article in a highly regarded journal than the sole author of a moderate article in a publication with only a modest reputation.

Wherever you send it, make sure you 'survey the terrain' beforehand and familiarise yourself with your chosen journal's style, focus, structure and content by looking at previous editions (see Lunt and Davidson, 2000, for a thorough discussion on publishing in journals).

In the hierarchy of academic appraisal, an article in a refereed journal counts for more than a chapter contributed to a multi-author book. Nonetheless, only a very confident new researcher would turn down an invitation to contribute to such a collection; most would, rightly, take the chance to become better known in their chosen field. Multi-author books often stem from conferences, and your chances of being invited to contribute will be enhanced by giving the editor of the volume-to-be the impression of enthusiasm, efficiency and punctuality. You should also enrol your supervisor and other well-disposed senior colleagues as advocates for the inclusion of your piece. Some enterprising PhD students have jointly compiled multi-author volumes of their own (see 'Books' below).

On the whole, journal and multi-author book editors will be looking for clearly structured and well argued pieces of work. If you have managed to identify a 'gap' in the literature on your topic, this would obviously be an ideal theme around which to build the article. You can draw on and use the wide literature review you have already undertaken as a way of indicating how others have argued, before pointing out the deficits of particular approaches. Your supervisor ought to be able to advise you on the content and structure of a possible article submission.

Books

For job prospects in academia it is incredibly helpful to have had your PhD published. The period spent thinking, researching and writing a doctoral thesis will be the longest, most undisturbed period of pure research you are likely to enjoy. It is therefore a waste *not* to publish the outcome in some form. Your external examiner in the viva is, in many cases, the one who can advise you on possibilities for publication, providing of course he or she is happy with what you have submitted. Nowadays it is becoming more difficult for specialist PhD-monographs to get published, as publishers increasingly turn away from these and look for textbook type manuscripts that are likely to have a bigger sale. However, it is well worth putting in a lot of effort to try to get a book based on your thesis published.

The best strategy would see you publish one or two articles from your PhD manuscript before it is published as a book. If you were to publish any more you would begin to cut your chances of finding anyone who would want to publish, or indeed buy, your book. Academic books or monographs are published by specialist publishing houses, or in specialised sections of general publishing houses. They are often published in series, editorially led by one, two or three important scholars, sometimes advised by a panel or editorial board of a dozen or so even more important scholars. Your chances of acceptance by the publisher are enormously enhanced if you are endorsed by a series editors or board member. This is where your supervisor can help – if you are lucky he or she may be one of these important people; if not, he or she probably knows one or two of them. Exploit these connections. Make sure you are told when publishers' editors are visiting your department, and when you have a book plan (see below), arrange a meeting with the visitor.

Get to know the publishers and the series in your field. Look overseas – many, probably most, English-language books are published by non-UK houses. The USA is home to the largest academic community in the world, and boasts hundreds of academic publishers, including literally scores of university presses. Bear in mind that English-language scholarly books are published in all the north-western European countries, as well, of course, as in all the English-speaking countries. You should aim to be familiar with all the publishers in your field – examine the first few pages (the 'prelims') of the books in your section of the library, read publishers' catalogues, surf the net, always make a note of the name and address of the publisher of any books you cite or find in other bibliographies. Three invaluable reference books for aspiring academic authors are the *Association of American University Presses Directory (AAUP)*, published by Chicago University Press, the *Literary Market Place* (for North American publishers) and *International Literary Market Place* (for the rest of the world), both published by Bowker. The AAUP directory is absurdly cheap: every academic library should hold a recent edition; the Bowker books are huge, and hugely expensive.

Most of the time book publishers base their first and most important decision (reject it now or give it a chance) on book plans (also called outlines, proposals or synopses). They do not welcome and will not read unsolicited theses. Most academic publishers state that they will not publish theses or collected volumes. None the less, all academic publishers' lists continue to feature books by many hands, and books closely based on theses. The authors or compilers of these books made the breakthrough by putting in front of the publisher a good, detailed, fitting and scholarly outline. Every academic publisher will tell you, if you care to ask, what they look for in a book outline. Find out from their catalogue or Website, or their representative, face-to-face or by email; then follow their preferences.

Broadly speaking, a PhD manuscript is written for a different purpose than a book, and may legitimately contain multiple repetition, the constant reaffirming of central hypotheses, all within the peculiar structure of a doctoral thesis. Usually, publishers want the section you have agonised over most, the theoretical chapter, to be reduced, simplified and made more reader-friendly. They will also be looking for a more inclusive approach to others' published work – quotation and paraphrase, not citation – as part of a broadening of treatment. Most publishers have a specific book proposal form, usually available on the Web, on which you can submit your ideas. Obtain a proposal form and study the questions the publisher asks. Be prepared to demonstrate a number of things, including why your book is so great, the market for the book (i.e. the people who are likely to buy it), and how it differs from other books on your topic currently on the market.

Ethics and plagiarism in research

Ethics

Ethics impact on all forms of social research. A researcher has a set of moral principles that guide him or her in their choice of how to conduct themselves with regard to such topics as confidentiality, anonymity, legality, professionalism and privacy when dealing with people in research (Blaxter *et al.*, 1997, 148). As a researcher you have a duty to respect the people you are studying and you need to make sure you ask their explicit permission first, and then make very clear how you intend to collect, analyse and disseminate the data you have gathered by talking to them.

There are a number of professional organisations that set out explicit ethical codes for researchers (for the web-site addresses see Bryman, 2001, 476). These can be a useful starting point for new researchers, for the topic of ethics is not clear-cut, as one person's ethical behaviour may not equate to another person's. Although you may not consider that ethics play much of a role in your research, you do need to reflect on a few things, especially if you intend working with qualitative methods, because

> While all social research intrudes to some extent in people's lives, qualitative research often intrudes more. Some qualitative research deals with the most sensitive, intimate and innermost matters in people's lives, and ethical issues inevitably accompany the collection of such information. (Punch, 2000a, 281)

Punch sums up the main areas in which ethical issues can arise in research as:

- harm
- consent
- deception
- privacy
- confidentiality.

You need to consider the likelihood of your research actually *harming* the people who participate in it. This may be difficult to assess, as the impact may be psychological, especially if you are asking people about a traumatic incident in their past.

Another key issue is that of the lack of informed consent. This issue was brought to the public's attention recently by a news reporter who used covert tactics to infiltrate specific groups in society, most notoriously a violent football hooligan gang. The use of covert cameras and the lack of the participants' consent – however much we may dislike them – is an ethical issue. However, in some cases it may be desirable to actually participate in direct observation *without* the group you are observing actually knowing who you are or what you are doing, as this would, arguably, affect the way they behave in their 'natural setting'. The line between what is ethically acceptable and what is not is very difficult to establish.

The same goes for certain forms of deception in research. By 'deception' we mean the situation in which researchers deliberately give false information to respondents in order to elicit a particular response.

The most famous case of this was the ethically dubious study carried out by Stanley Milgram in 1963, in which participants were deceived into believing that they were administering electric shocks to experimental subjects who answered questions wrongly (see Bryman, 2001, 477, for a summary of this case). Other studies use an (acceptable?) element of deception, for example, by dressing the researcher as a figure of authority to elicit and record a particular response from people. In this case it would obviously be counterproductive to explain to each and every person you meet what your research is about (see ibid. 484).

Respecting a person's privacy and confidentiality is also an ethical issue. If you interview someone and promise not to print their personal details, you must keep to that promise. First, because you would have otherwise deceived the person, which in itself is reprehensible, but second, you will tarnish the reputation of research in general. This is particularly important in the case of an interview with a person whom researchers after you may wish to meet. Once lied to, the subject is much less likely to give another researcher an interview.

Finally, the way in which you conduct your research, collect your data, analyse it and disseminate it all impact on ethical issues. You *must* avoid using sloppy research techniques, misinterpreting data, drawing conclusions from insufficient data and deliberately misrepresenting findings. The latter is enough to see you excluded from consideration for any serious academic post for the rest of your working life.

Plagiarism

Plagiarism is a well-known term, but an extremely hard one to define in practice. The original meaning of the term was 'kidnapping', although it has now come to mean the act of stealing *or presenting as one's own*, the ideas or work of someone else.

Make sure that you obtain your institution's guidelines on plagiarism at the earliest possible opportunity. Ben Rosamond (2001, 1–4), in one of the few illuminating pieces on this topic, rightly points out the differences in definitions of this term and what exactly constitutes an act of plagiarism. He goes on to outline four ways in which plagiarism is generally understood:

1. Plagiarism reflects shoddy scholarship and the failure to meet the exacting standards expected in academic life.
2. Plagiarism is seen as an infringement of the informal practices that

allow academic life to proceed, that is, a breakdown of trust between teacher and student, and among students themselves.

3. A further approach is to see the act of plagiarism as actually breaching ethical codes and standards.

4. The final way of looking at plagiarism is to see it in legal terms of a breach of copyright and a form of fraud. This includes the violation of the intellectual property of an original author of the piece of work plagiarised. Akin to this is the notion of 'stealing' people's ideas and passing them off as your own, effectively reaping what you did not sow.

The explosion of Web-based activities has boosted the potential for plagiarism to an extent that is very difficult to estimate. With Websites specifically focusing on offering academic essays which can be purchased by credit card, the chances of cheating have greatly increased, while the chances of catching blatant cheats have greatly diminished. The fact that students at undergraduate and taught-graduate level routinely prepare their essays on computers and submit them electronically has greatly increased the opportunities for plagiarism.

Make sure that you cite the exact Website and date, if you use any material from the web. As the use of the internet grows, and important institutions such as the Massachusetts Institute of Technology (MIT) begin the process of offering *all their course packs* freely available through the internet (Guardian, 2001), the tricky question of what constitutes plagiarism will increase in complexity.

As Rosamond rightly points out, the temptation to cheat is usually greater as deadlines loom and funding dries up. Learn good time-management skills from the start and avoid including anything in your thesis that you cannot honestly account for. To guard yourself further against accusations of plagiarism familiarise yourself with the referencing conventions of your discipline and get into the habit of making a detailed note of books, articles and journals you have taken information from. There is an increasing need to protect yourself against accusations of plagiarism, especially in the light of strict ownership of data, copyright and intellectual property rights laws.

Training and dissemination

Postgraduate research training

With the emphasis increasingly on the period of time students have to complete their doctorates and the regulations set out by the key funding bodies, postgraduate research training is becoming more and more central to doctoral studies. The advice offered here is on how you can actually enjoy it; how to get the most out of this (compulsory) training and why you should see it as an advantage and not as an extra load to be dragged along the road to completion.

There are, generally speaking, three distinct approaches adopted by postgraduate students to the study of methods and methodology. The first is the 'just in case' approach, whereby a student attempts to obtain a complete and comprehensive grasp of *all* methodological approaches in the field of social science. This course of action usually leads to a student being a jack of all trades and master of none. Whilst it is a good idea to be aware of debates and approaches in fields other than your own, you must master those most relevant to your topic first.

Second, there is the 'just in time' approach to the study of methods and methodology, a course of action which sees the student attempting to pick up certain skills as and when they need them, with the result that some stages of the research process cannot be undertaken until the requisite skills are acquired. At first glance this approach may sound sensible, however, under the stringent time conditions of postgraduate research, any miscalculations on the time it takes to master fully, for example, a statistical package will impact directly on the time available to complete the thesis.

The final approach, and the one recommended here, is the 'just for you' approach. After learning the fundamentals of research, so that you no longer struggle to penetrate the terms and terminology of research methods courses, turn your mind and energy towards the actual content of your course. In order to get the most out of such a course, the 'just for you' approach proposes:

- As far as is possible, gear all of the assignments or assessments towards what you need to do in your own thesis. Most of the apathy associated with research methods courses can be traced back to the fact that students do not see the *point* in undertaking a particular exercise. If you can relate an assignment directly to your work, you are more likely to apply yourself wholeheartedly.

- Actively use the course convenor as another feedback channel by getting them to read through your methods or methodological section, then discuss any comments they make with your supervisor.
- Engage with methods that you are *not* employing in your thesis. Try to understand their philosophical underpinnings. For example, if you hate qualitative research and have no intention of doing it, attempt to understand *why* it is looked upon as useful. The same goes for quantitative research. The point is that the best researcher is the one who has an *understanding* of the logic, rationale, philosophy and utility of both types of research, be they associated with discipline X or discipline Y. Equally, you will be in a good position to justify your choice of methods in your work.

Seminars, conferences and workshops

Academic gatherings, such as workshops and conferences, offer you the ideal chance to implement some of the key issues touched on above. The best advice is to use seminars, conferences and workshops in a constructive manner for the progression, presentation and dissemination of your work and for networking with others in your field. You need to strike a balance between the perpetual conference-goer who knows and networks with everybody but is not known for his or her work, and someone who never attends, because he or she is too busy working.

If giving a paper fills you with dread, brings you out in a cold sweat and reduces you to a bag of nerves, there are two solutions: (a) opt for a career other than academia, or (b) practise as much as you can by giving lots of papers. Practice is the key to success, because by practising the art of paper-giving, you can actually come to like it. You should always ensure a modicum of eye-contact with the audience (there is nothing worse than looking at the top of someone's head for half an hour), ensure you are not trying to pack too much into too little space of time, and print out the text in a large enough size to be able to read it with ease.

Seminars

Presenting your work in, or simply attending, any one of the formats suggested here can be very beneficial to your work. However, they differ slightly in their purpose and in the way they may be of benefit to your studies. A seminar can take various forms. An open seminar, to which an outside expert is invited to speak, will be useful to the novice as a way of watching a more established academic set out his or her arguments. You should listen carefully – regardless of the subject matter – to the manner in which the speaker sets up questions, goes about answering them (or not) and the methods by which they arrive at these answers. Do not be surprised if many senior academics cannot tell the difference between methods and methodology. However, resist the temptation of becoming another conference hack, but rather engage with the core of the presentation: How were the key concepts defined? Was there any relation between the theoretical approach outlined and the actual data presented?

Watching a more experienced peer deliver a paper on work-in-progress is possibly one of the most useful exercises for new postgraduates. Look and listen carefully at the way they use, define and operationalise concepts and think about some of the key issues discussed in this book: Is there a clear question–method match? What about the theory–empirical match? Is there a logical and structured argument in the presentation? Are they using concepts and terms in the appropriate way? (You will be surprised how many people use ideal types, typologies and paradigms interchangeably, simply assuming they all mean the same thing.) The point here is not to make yourself extremely unpopular by pointing out such misuses of terms, but to observe how others who have progressed further along the research process than you prepare and deliver a summarised version of their topics.

A seminar at which you are giving the paper and at which you are the centre of attention is, of course, a different matter. You now move from the passive, and easier, role of commentator or critic to the producer and presenter. The boot is now clearly on the other foot, and peers and staff members will be looking for cracks in your arguments or your misuse of terms and concepts. Remember *not* to try and pack everything into a seminar paper, as the result will be a mad rush towards the end, an even more nervous presenter and the possibility of having to leave out the most significant section.

A good idea for a first seminar paper is simply to outline your proposed topic. This gives you a number of advantages over a normal seminar paper: (a) you have a fairly structured paper before you start, and (b) you are only *proposing* to do what you are presenting, and you are open to suggestions on how to improve it. If we return to the standard example of the structure of an MPhil or PhD I proposed in chapter one, it should look broadly like this:

- introduction
- literature review
- methodology (ontology/epistemology)

- case study(ies)/empirical section
- evaluation
- conclusion/further work.

You could either touch on each stage of the thesis and suggest what you intend to do, including highlighting some tentative 'hunches' you might have, or you may prefer to concentrate on one particular aspect, say, the methodology section. You could then break this down into an approach, the research questions or hypotheses, and possible levels and units of analysis, and mention the case study or research site. Additionally, you could outline some of the types of method you wish to employ – more experienced students and staff will have had first-hand experience with a variety of methods and their feedback will be invaluable. Whatever you choose to present, make sure you write down *all* comments, whether they seem right, wrong or uninteresting, and you can go over them under more reflective circumstances after the seminar. Whatever topic you present on, go in prepared. Find out exactly how long you have to speak, check out the room in which you will speak and find out who the audience is likely to consist of, as this may affect the content or delivery of your talk.

Conferences and workshops
Conferences and workshops differ in the manner in which they are run, the rationale behind their being held, and their use to the student. Conferences are larger, nearly always attended by a great number of delegates. They range from a straightforward one-day conference with perhaps ten speakers to huge affairs with eight or more parallel sessions running at any one time. The latter is usually a place to go to mingle, network and get to know others in your field. Delivering a conference paper will differ from the seminar paper in so far as you will not see the friendly faces of your own faculty but rather a room full of strangers, who may well be from a wide variety of disciplines. If this is so, you are bound to receive questions couched in unfamiliar terms or discourse peculiar to a particular discipline. Being aware of the fact that such differences exist will prepare you and lessen the shock. Also, it is unlikely that the conference organisers will have asked you to present an outline of your project. Most conferences are loosely based around a theme which is tightened somewhat around panels, so that your topic will have to fit with one of the panels. Unless you have been active in a research environment prior to embarking on a higher degree, it is unlikely that you will deliver such a paper until either the end of an MPhil or the second year of a PhD.

The exception to the above is, of course, the growing number of 'graduate networks' springing up under the auspices of major professional academic associations. My advice is to look up and join such a graduate network in your or a neighbouring field as soon as you begin your studies. The networking effects of such organisations help to combat the feeling of isolation that many doctoral students suffer from. They also allow an interface with the 'grown-up' version of the organisation and facilitate the transition from student to professional academic at a later stage.

A workshop is usually a cosier affair than a conference, with the day being organised around a relatively narrow theme. There are a wide variety of formats that can be used in workshops – as with conferences. The currently favoured arrangement seems to be a number of short papers (usually restricted to a maximum of 15–20 minutes) followed by a generous amount of time for discussion and questions. At the end of the workshop it is usual to have some form of plenary session or round-table at which many of the core and recurring themes of the day are drawn together and summarised.

The end-product of these types of workshop, and sometimes of conferences or conference panels, may be a book or special edition of a journal. You will benefit from joining in this publication, though you normally have to be invited. Maximise your chances by appearing coherent, sober and reliable at all times during the meeting. If there is a group organised around a theme or topic close to your own, then enquire about how you can join, as this is an ideal forum to present nascent ideas to those actually interested in your topic.

The utility of a PhD

This final section sums up the utility of the modern research-based postgraduate degree. It outlines the essential factors that you need to undertake postgraduate research and those which you should learn or enhance during the process. They consist of a number of general skills and many more employment-related, or transferable, skills than you would at first imagine. Long gone are the days when the true image of a research student was that of a loner with limited interpersonal skills, and no practical skills to speak of.

Timekeeping skills

If you can meet the deadlines you and others have set, especially under the psychological pressure of doing a doctorate, and finish your work within three years, you indicate to employers a clear grasp of timekeeping skills and the ability to *manage* and *prioritise* a huge amount of information and condense it into an intelligible and coherent text. All of these points are particularly attractive to prospective employers, because you will have had to make quick, and often difficult, decisions under intense time constraints.

Communication skills

Communication skills come in many forms: writing skills will be developed over the course of your studies, especially if you engage in writing for publication and writing conference papers and reports from fieldwork. All of these activities demand and enhance different types of writing skills. In all written work aim for clarity over complexity. Oral skills will also develop as you become used to engaging and interacting with other students and academics. The dissemination of your own work, both oral and written, will develop and improve as you learn the discourse of your particular discipline and the terms of generic research skills and methods.

Teamwork and networking skills

To avoid isolation and to gain valuable experience in working with others, use every opportunity to get involved in organising conferences or workshops in your department, faculty or school. Working in a team can promote the ability to see things from others' point of view – not a bad idea for researchers – learning to compromise and experiencing the mutual benefit of the pooling of joint resources. Networking is another useful skill, but it is much more difficult to learn. There is more than one way to network: there are those who can naturally mingle and make connections, who know a lot of people, but who do not go out of their way to network. They would not betray their own fundamental principles in order to get a visiting card from Professor Bloggs. On the other hand, there are those who seem to be out just to network. Their existence revolves around conferences, workshops and general networking events. Not many people know what they *actually* do, but they do know *of* them. You should aim to network with people *who are of genuine intellectual interest to you*. There is a fine balance to be found between positive self-promotion and the marketing of your ideas, on the one hand, and coming across as an egoist out to further his or her career in any way possible, on the other.

IT skills

By the end of your studies, you are likely to be highly skilled in the use of an advanced word-processing package, the Internet, e-mail and the library bibliographical system. In addition, you may have learned Excel spreadsheets or a package like SPSS. All of these skills will be of use (a) when you begin looking for a job, especially those posted on the Web, and (b) in getting you a job.

Teaching

Gaining experience in teaching during your studies is recommended, as it is often a requirement for academic posts. It will also be beneficial to you in other ways: first, it is a good way of finding out if academia is really for you; second, the experience of having to condense vast amounts of information into digestible chunks will be useful in your own research and writing work; third, if it works out well, it can be a boost to your confidence and even turn out to be an enjoyable event. Finally, your communication skills should develop as a result of teaching, the point of it is to impart complex information clearly and economically to others, after all.

All in all, postgraduate research can provide you with a set of skills, experiences and knowledge that will be of benefit to you for the rest of your life whatever profession you choose to pursue.

Summary

The final chapter has surveyed some of the most important aspects of doctoral research, especially supervision, the viva and ethical matters. To sum up the key points:

- Remember to play a proactive role in the student–supervisor relationship.
- Get the most out of supervisions by preparing for them and submitting written work prior to meetings.
- Find other people with whom you can discuss your work and who can give you feedback on written work.

- Prepare for your viva by learning the tools and terminology of research.
- Be prepared for sustained questioning on your methodological approach, your use of qualitative or quantitative research, the sources you have drawn on and the generalisablity of your findings.
- Ensure your thesis has a good question–method match and a logical coherence between the respective sections, especially the theoretical and empirical.
- Listen very carefully to the examiners' questions and be prepared to take on board criticism.
- Reflect on the ethics of your research and take great care to record *all* secondary sources and cite them properly.
- Use your research training actively to your advantage and learn *why* researchers choose specific methods.
- Go to conferences, workshops and seminars and use them to learn from, observe others and deliver your own ideas
- Use your period of study to build up a portfolio of employment-related skills.

Further reading:

Blaxter, L., Hughes, C. and Tight, M. (1997) *How to Research,* Buckingham, Open University Press, chapters 6 and 8.

Bryman, A. (2001) *Social Research Methods,* Oxford, Oxford University Press, chapter 24.

Burnham, P. (1997) 'Surviving the Viva', in: Burnham, P. (ed.) *Surviving the Research Process in Politics,* London/Washington, Pinter.

Delamont, S., Atkinson, P. and Parry, O. (1999) *Supervising the PhD. A Guide to Success,* Buckingham/Philadelphia, SRHE and Open University Press, chapter 8.

Fairbairn, G. J. and Winch, C. (2000) *Reading, Writing and Reasoning. A Guide for Students,* Buckingham/Philadelphia, Open University Press, 2nd Edition, sections 1.3–2.3.

Graves, N. (1999) 'Problems of Supervision', in: Graves, N. and Varma, V. (eds.) *Working for a Doctorate: A Guide for Humanities and Social Sciences,* London/New York, Routledge.

Hartley, J. (1999) 'Writing the Thesis', in: Graves and Varma (eds.) *Working for a Doctorate: A Guide for Humanities and Social Sciences*, London/New York, Routledge.

Lunt, N. and Davidson, C. (2000) 'Journey to the Centre of the (Academic) Universe: 20 Steps on Getting Published in Journals' in: *Politics*, 20 (1): 43–50.

Phillips, E. M. and Pugh, D. S. (eds.) (1994) *How to Get a PhD. A Handbook for Students and Their Supervisors*, Buckingham/Philadelphia, Open University Press, chapter 8.

Rosamond, B. (2001) 'Plagiarism, Academic Norms and the Governance of the Profession', unpublished manuscript.

Silverman, D. (2000) *Doing Qualitative Research. A Practical Handbook*, London/Thousand Oaks/New Delhi, Sage, chapters 4 and 22.

Van Evera, S. (1997) *Guide to Methods for Students of Political Science*, Ithaca NY/London, Cornell University Press, chapter 4.

Appendix 1:
Glossary of research terms

The following glossary of terms lists the words marked in bold throughout the main text. In some cases I have consulted etymological dictionaries in order to give the underlying meaning and origin of words, as going back to the roots of many terms is a good way of getting under the cloak of complexity surrounding them. Most of the following words are either explained in the main text or their meanings are obvious from the context in which they have been used. The best idea is to look at both the glossary *and* the word or term in the text to get a better understanding of it.

Approach
An approach describes the method used or steps taken in setting about a task or problem, especially with reference to which means of access or which sources are to be employed. Approaches are, like **methodologies**, particular ways of producing or getting at knowledge and as such are very much dependent on the view of the world taken by those that use them, or to put it technically, they are informed by the paradigmatic assumptions upon which they are based. For example, a neoliberal approach to international relations would be underpinned by specific **ontological** and **epistemological** assumptions which would not necessarily be shared by other approaches to the same subject of enquiry in the same field.

Case study
Case studies are a very popular way of structuring projects. A case study is a restriction or narrowing of focus to one or more towns, individuals, organisations, etc., which are studied in great detail. Usually a variety of **quantitative** and **qualitative** research methods are used within case-study approaches, with the aim of shedding light on the object of study. Case studies are an example of a specific *type* of approach. They represent par-

ticular strategies for research, involving empirical investigation of a particular contemporary phenomenon within its real-life context, and employing multiple sources of evidence.

Causal/causality

Causation refers to the process of one event causing or producing another event (often referred to as 'cause and effect'). A causal relationship between two **variables** or things, for example, smoking and major diseases, is much clearer, and far less speculative, than a correlation between two variables or things. A great deal of **quantitative research**, and some **qualitative research**, attempts to identify causal relationships among the variables employed in the study.

Concept

The original meaning of the Latin term *conceptus* was 'a collecting, gathering or conceiving'. The modern-day equivalent encapsulates these sentiments. A concept is a general notion or an idea expressed in words or as a symbol. Concepts, like **theories**, range from the very simple to the complex, from the very specific to the highly abstract and are regarded as the building blocks of theory (Blaikie, 2000, 129). When concepts are **operationalised** in such a manner that they can be 'measured' to take on different numerical values, they are referred to as variables (Rudestam and Newton, 1992, 19). Cross-border co-operation is a concept which sums up a wide variety of transboundary interaction. In a project, this concept would have to be unpacked, clarified and limited in order to make it understandable to the reader and operationalisable in research.

Conceptual framework

This is an analytical tool providing a broad language and form of reference in which reality can be examined. Conceptual frameworks go even further than static models and **ideal types** by offering interpretations of relationships between events and **variables**.

Correlation

Correlation is the term used for any significant association (or covariation) between two or more **variables**. Importantly, correlation *does not mean nor imply* causation (Landman, 2000, 224, my emphasis).

Data collection

Data collection is the process through which **empirical** data are produced and collected via a number of different data sources. There are many different methods of data collection, both **quantitative** and **qualitative**, and a wide range of sources of data that can be collected.

Deductive research

Research which begins with clear assumptions or previous knowledge in order to understand a particular problem or find the answer to a problem. Above all, it is a label given to theory-driven research as opposed to research that seeks to derive **theories** from **empirical** evidence (see **inductive research**). The term 'hypothetico-deductive' is reserved for such research that relates to or makes use of the method of proposing **hypotheses** and testing their acceptability or falsity by checking their logical consequences are consistent with empirical data (see the Encyclopedia Britannica on-line).

Dependent variable

The thing which is caused or affected by the **independent variable**. In the example in the text of chapter 3, the dependent variable was deeper European integration, which was facilitated by the independent variable of cross-border co-operation. The dependent variable is also known as the outcome variable, endogenous variable or the explanandum (Landman, 2000, 224–5). It is important to remember that every dependent variable can also be an independent variable: it is the researcher who chooses.

Dissertation

In the UK it is usual to use the term 'dissertation' for a relatively long piece of work over and above the length of an extended essay. Students studying for a first degree or MA usually complete a dissertation as opposed to a **thesis** (see below). To add to the confusion, the term 'dissertation' is used in other countries such as Germany to refer to a doctoral **thesis**.

Empirical

From the Latin *empiricus*, meaning 'experience', empirical has come to mean the opposite of theoretical, that is, that which is derived from, guided by or based on observation, experiments or experience rather than ideas or **theories**. Many philosophical positions and **approaches** have been built up around empiricism, the core belief of which is that all knowledge is derived from sense-experience as opposed to learning through rational thinking. The term is generally used in combinations such as: empirical evidence; empirical data; empirical (as opposed to theoretical) study or research and empirical knowledge.

Epistemology
Derived from the Greek words *episteme* (knowledge) and *logos* (reason), epistemology is the **theory** of knowledge. Epistemological considerations depend on beliefs about the nature of knowledge. Also, assumptions about forms of knowledge, access to knowledge and ways of acquiring and gathering knowledge are epistemological issues (Holloway, 1997, 54). All of the above impact on the research process and, importantly, **data collection** and analysis. Epistemology refers to the 'strategies through which a particular theory gathers knowledge and ensures that its reading of phenomena is superior to rival theories' (Rosamond, 2000, 7, 199).

Ethnographic research
From the noun 'ethnography', the original meaning of which was 'the description of races', ethnographical research is characterised by long stays in the field in which the researcher submerges himself or herself in the culture, language and day-to-day lives of those they are studying. The aim is to find patterns of power between specific group-members, study symbols of identity formation, the use of language, and so on.

Evaluation
The evaluation of data is one of the last stages of research, in which the researcher determines the significance, value and utility of his or her findings by careful and systematic analysis. At this stage, data are usually coded or categorised to assist the process.

Fieldwork
The activity of **data collection**: a term related to the **empirical** side of research in which data are gathered on site or on location. It usually involves spending a sustained amount of time at the area under study, or in archives, or interviewing. During fieldwork, data are gathered with which to observe relationships between certain selected **variables**, or new relationships and variables may be found.

Grounded theory
Grounded theory, a phrase coined by B. G. Glaser and A. L. Strauss in the 1960s, refers to a research strategy that does not start with a **hypothesis**, but rather seeks relationships between concepts once the data have been collected. This type of research involves the interpretation of data in their social and cultural contexts (see Holloway, 80–87).

Hermeneutics

Hermeneutics pertains to interpretation and can be understood as a form of data analysis which seeks to analyse a text from the perspective of the person who penned it, whilst emphasising the social and historical context within which it was produced.

Heuristic tool

Heuristic is an adjective that basically means 'involving or serving as an aid to discovering or learning', in particular by trial-and-error methods. Heuristic research tools are conceptual devices that help the researcher to obtain specific information. One example of this is Weber's **Ideal type**.

Hypothesis

A hypothesis is a proposition, set of propositions or assumption put forward for **empirical** testing; a testable proposition about the relationship between two or more events or **concepts**. Hypotheses are traditionally linked to the *deductive* method of research, whereby such propositions are derived from theory to provide the 'why' questions in social research (Blaikie, 2000, 163). A hypothesis consists of an **independent** and **dependent variable** and contains a **causal** proposition.

Ideal type

An ideal type is a construct – a description of a phenomenon in its abstract form which can assist in comparing and classifying specific phenomena (Holloway, 1997, 90). Our conference hack introduced in chapter 2 is an abstract notion of a person who exhibits specific characteristics; we can compare reality against this abstract notion. However, the example given of a know-all who talks a great deal and publishes little does not adequately deal with the kind of conference hack who obscures a lack of knowledge by continuous emphasis of ontological and epistemological questions, but who *has* in fact published a great deal, albeit in a different field. Hence one would have to adapt the ideal type in categorising the latter case.

Independent variable

See **dependent variable**. Shown as 'X' in formal models, the independent variable is also known as a causal variable, an explanatory variable, an exogenous variable, or the explicandum (Landman, 2000, 226).

Inductive research

Induction is, broadly, a mode of reasoning from the particular to the general, and inductive research can be understood as research which draws conclusions from specific **empirical** data (the particular) and attempts to generalise from them (the general), leading to more abstract ideas, including **theories**.

Inference

Both **quantitative** and **qualitative research** use inference. The act of inferring involves passing from one proposition or statement considered true, to another whose truth is believed to follow from that of the former. Inference can be by deductive or inductive methods and is particularly used in connection with statistical calculations, with which the researcher attempts to extrapolate from sample data to generalisations (see Encyclopedia Britannica on-line).

Literature review (otherwise known as a review of the literature or literature survey)

Usually one of the first steps in the research process is a review of the literature on and around the subject of enquiry. Its main functions are to avoid duplication, 'discover' gaps in research (or areas to which you can add knowledge) and 'place' your own approach among the work and approaches of other scholars. In this book I have highlighted three types of literature review: the initial 'dip' stage; the second review in which research questions and/or **hypotheses** are developed and defined and the final 'critical literature review'.

Macro

Macro means 'long' or 'large' in Greek and, in social research, pertains to a level of analysis which focuses on countries, systems, structures, institutions and organisations as opposed to individual actors.

Methodology

Methodology is a branch of science concerned with methods and techniques of scientific enquiry; in particular, with investigating the potential and limitations of particular techniques or procedures. The term pertains to the science and study of methods and the assumptions about the ways in which knowledge is produced. A certain methodological approach will be underpinned by and reflect specific **ontological** and **epistemological** assumptions. These assumptions will determine the *choice* of approach and methods adopted in a given study by emphasising particular ways of knowing and finding out about the world. Methodology deals with the logic of enquiry, of how **theories** can be generated and subsequently tested. Methodology is *very* often confused and used interchangeably with **methods**.

Methods

The original Greek meaning of method was 'the pursuit of knowledge'. In a sense, this is still what it means in research today, in as much as the methods a researcher employs in a study, that is, the techniques and procedures used to collect and analyse data, are the tools with which we pursue knowledge. There is a wide variety of methods, ranging from discourse analysis, archival retrieval of data, interviews, direct observation, comparisons of data, and documentary analysis to surveys, questionnaires and statistics. Certain methods can be used in either **qualitative** or **quantitative research**. Although there is a general and artificial division between both types of approach, the best social science research is often carried out using a combination of both. The methods employed in a project are usually informed by the methodology chosen and the questions asked, rather than the other way around.

Micro

The original Greek meaning is 'small' and, in social research, 'micro' tends to refer to a level of analysis that includes the study of individuals as opposed to institutions and organisations.

Model

Models are replications of reality. Toy cars are models of the real thing on a smaller scale; in social science, researchers try to construct a simplification of reality by setting out models that indicate links between specific components. Models can be succinctly described as 'representations or stylised, simplified pictures of reality. They identify important components of a system but do not posit relationships among variables' (Stoker, 1995, 17–18).

Ontology

Ontology is a branch of metaphysics concerned with the nature of being. It can be understood as the basic image of social reality upon which a theory is based. Ontology relates to the way in which an individual views the world. Their ontological position is their 'answer to the question: what is the nature of the social and political reality to be investigated?' (Hay, 2002, 3), an assumption which is difficult if not impossible to refute empirically (ibid., 4). Your ontology is linked to the ways of enquiring and gathering knowledge, or your **epistemology**, which, in turn, is linked to your **methodology**. Thus the latter is rooted in your ontological position. The cave dwellers in Plato's example have a different view of social reality to those people on the outside of the cave (see chapter 2 for the full example).

Operationalise

To operationalise a **concept** is simply to turn it into a **variable** which can be 'measured' in **fieldwork** or in the gathering of information. The first stage is to develop or find a suitable concept that can be turned into a variable. Then we need to translate these abstract notions into something which can record or 'measure' data. In studies of democracies, for example, the concept of political engagement could be used to gauge the civic vibrancy of a region. We would need to find a suitable variable for this concept, for example, voting levels or membership figures of political parties or associations. We would thus have 'operationalised' the concept of political engagement in research.

Paradigm

Originally meaning 'pattern' or 'model', paradigm has come to mean, broadly, 'an established academic approach' in a specific discipline in which academics use a common terminology, common **theories** based on agreed paradigmatic assumptions and agreed **methods** and practices (see Rosamond, 2000, 192). Paradigms, which act as organising frameworks for researchers, are often overtaken or replaced by others, leading to what is commonly called a 'paradigm shift', that is, the former majority approach is superseded by a new approach, using different terminology, theories, **methods** and practices.

Parsimony

A parsimonious explanation is considered to be one which 'uses the least amount of evidence to explain the most amount of variation' (Landman, 2000, 227).

Qualitative research
Qualitative is derived from 'quality', a term coined by Plato to mean 'of what kind'. Qualitative research is characterised by methods that attempt to examine 'inherent traits, characteristics, and qualities of the political objects of inquiry' (Landman, 2000, 227). The **methods** used in this type of research tend to be more interpretative in nature.

Quantitative research
This term is derived from 'quantity', and pertains to numbers. Quantitative research employs methods with the intention of being able to produce data that can be quantified (counted, measured, weighed, enumerated, and so manipulated and compared mathematically). This type of research is interested in finding general patterns and relationships among **variables**, testing **theories** and making predictions (Ragin, 1994, 132–6).

Research questions
Research questions are intended to guide your enquiries. By establishing general research questions, the researcher begins to narrow his or her focus of enquiry, something that is essential given the amount of information available. A general research question would need to be answerable, for example, 'Does the fact that students have to take term-time jobs to subsist impact on their examination performance'? The next stage is to develop more specific research questions and, if appropriate, **hypotheses**. The former would sharpen the study's focus even more, while the latter would give you a (causal) statement to guide your studies, for example, 'Full-time students of economics who take term-time jobs perform worse than those economics students who do not', i.e. working in term-time jobs *is the cause of* the poor results.

Research strategy
A research strategy is the manner in which you approach your research topic, for example, inductively or deductively. This choice will impact on how you formulate your **research questions** or **hypotheses**, the level and units of analysis you choose and the type of study and the sources of data to be collected.

Sources
Sources are crucial to the research process. They represent the evidence with which to test **theories**, propositions, hunches, and so on. Without **empirical** evidence in the form of, for example, documents, statistics, interview transcripts etc., **hypotheses** in the social sciences would remain

untested, an unsatisfactory state of affairs unless the purpose of research was to contribute to theoretical debates. There is no general transdisciplinary consensus on the usefulness of some sources as opposed to others, as is the case with **methods, methodologies, approaches** and theories. However, the latter have a great impact on which sources the researcher will use. Generally, a wide source base will lessen the chance of an invalid study.

Structure and agency problem
This debate revolves around the puzzle of whether it is the social context in which individuals act that guides and determines their actions, or whether it is the individuals or 'actors' themselves who form and shape the social context and institutions around them. It has become customary in political science to establish a position on this, emphasising structure over agency or agency over structure, or sometimes a bit of both.

Theory
There are many different types of theory, ranging from grand and middle-range to **grounded theory**. (The difference between theories is their degree of abstraction and their scope. Grand theory is very abstract and presents a conceptual scheme 'intended to represent the important features of a total society' (Blaikie, 2000, 144). Middle-range theories, probably the most commonly used in research, are limited to a specific domain, for example, the labour process (Bryman, 2001, 6). For a definition of grounded theory see the entry in the glossary). A theory is a guess about the way things are. Theories are abstract notions which assert specific relationships between **concepts**. In research, theories are linked to *explanation* as opposed to *description*. The abstract ideas and propositions contained in theory are generally tested in **fieldwork** by the **collection of data**. A good theory will be generalisable and able to be employed in different contexts to the original. In the words of Karl Popper, theories are 'nets cast to catch what we call "the world": to rationalise, to explain and to master it. We endeavour to make the mesh ever finer and finer' (Popper, 2000, 59).

Thesis
A thesis is the large body of written work necessary for gaining a PhD or MPhil. The former usually requires a work of about 80,000 words, whereas the latter usually requires between 20,000 and 60,000 words.

Thick description

A detailed account of field experiences which contextualises and makes explicit the patterns of cultural and social relationships drawn from observations in the field. Thick description builds up a clear picture of the individuals and groups in the context of their culture and the setting in which they live (see Holloway, 1997, 154).

Triangulation

The term has come to be associated with the practice of drawing on a variety of data sources, which are cross-checked with one another to limit the chances of bias in the methods or sources employed. It is common practice to attempt to measure one particular **variable** using a variety of different methods, for example, mixing statistical analysis with **qualitative** methods to gain further insights into 'reality' on the ground. There is a difference between triangulating methods and the triangulation of data resulting from diverse sources.

Typology

The early Greek philosophers, Socrates, Plato and Aristotle, all used some form of categorisation. Today, a typology, like a taxonomy, can be seen as a classificatory system with which the researcher categorises data. These devices can be seen as loose frameworks with which to organise and systematise our observations. Like **ideal types**, typologies and taxonomies do not provide us with explanation, rather they describe and simplify empirical phenomena by fitting them into a set of categories.

Validating

Very similar in meaning to 'verify', *see* **verifiability of data**. In research, scholars attempt to achieve 'internal validity' and 'external validity' of their research. The former refers to the extent to which researchers can demonstrate that they have evidence for the statements and descriptions they make; the latter refers to a study's generalisability, that is, the relevance of the study's statements over and above the case study used (see Holloway, 1997, 159–62).

Value-free

This refers to the notion of value neutrality of researchers when investigating the social world, an ideal which has come to be seen as impossible in social science research, as all investigators have particular perspectives. However, as a scholar one should make the following *absolutely clear*: the choices of **theoretical** approaches, the **variables** used in the study and the research design and any limitations of the inferences from the work (see Landman, 2000, 51).

Variables
Variables are concepts which vary in amount or kind. Researchers **operationalise concepts** by translating them into variables that can be 'measured' and used in gathering information.

Verifiability of data
The verb to verify, means literally 'to prove to be true' or 'test the correctness, accuracy or reality of'. In research, one speaks of the verifiability of findings or data, that is, the ability to check the data a researcher has gathered by following the same methods or **data collection** and data-analysis techniques.

Viva (voce)
The viva voce, literally, the 'living voice', is an oral examination. For PhD students, and some MPhil students, it marks the culmination of their efforts and is a process carried out behind closed doors between the candidate, the internal and external examiners and perhaps a chairperson. If successful, the viva can be understood as a passage from a student to a professional 'Dr'. The title, however, is officially only allowed to be used after graduation.

Working hypothesis
A working hypothesis is a proposition which helps guide subsequent research and which can be defined and refined in the light of further research.

Appendix 2:
Examples of reference systems

The 'Harvard' method of referencing

This, perhaps the most commonly used system in journals, is an easy and efficient way of referencing your sources. The standard set-out is as follows:

> In the text you cite the author's name, the year of publication and, if you are referring to a specific passage or quotation, the page number. This is placed in brackets in the text: (Cooke, 2000, 43). In the bibliography or reference list, give the full bibliographical details of the text, that is, the author's name and initial, the year of publication, the book or article title, place of publication (usually a town) and the publisher.

For example:

Cooke, P. (2000) *Speaking the Taboo: a Study of the Work of Wolfgang Hilbig*, Amsterdam/Atlanta, Rodopi.

A note for purists: to be precise, the 'Harvard' system is just one example of a *Name–Date system*; however, the specific term has now almost completely displaced the general, as with 'Hoover' and 'vacuum cleaner'.

The 'Humanities' or 'numeric' method of referencing

The 'Humanities' method of referencing involves the citation of references by a superscript numeral in the text, with the full bibliographical details of the work given in the footnote text at the bottom of the page or in endnotes at the end of the section or chapter. The same information as in the example above needs to be given.

Whichever system you choose, keep with it throughout the whole text (see Fairbairn and Winch, 2000, 116–25 for a full discussion on referencing).

Bibliography

Bartov, V. (1997) 'Research Design – "A Rough Guide"', in: Burnham, P. (ed.) *Surviving the Research Process in Politics,* London/Washington, Pinter.

Bell, J. (1993) *Doing Your Research Project. A Guide to First-Time Researchers in Education and Social Science,* Buckingham, Open University Press.

Blaikie, N. (2000) *Designing Social Research,* Cambridge, Polity Press.

Blaxter, L., Hughes, C. and Tight, M. (1997) *How to Research,* Buckingham, Open University Press.

Bouma, G. D. and Atkinson, G. B. J. (1995) *A Handbook of Social Research. A Comprehensive and Practical Guide for Students,* New York, Oxford University Press.

Brown, G. and Atkins, M. (1993) *Effective Teaching in Higher Education,* London, Routledge.

Bryman, A. (1995) *Research Methods and Organization Studies,* London/New York, Routledge.

Bryman, A. (2001) *Social Research Methods,* Oxford, Oxford University Press.

Bryman, A. and Cramer, D. (1994) *Analysis for Social Scientists,* London, Routledge, revised edition.

Burnham, P. (1997) 'Surviving the Viva', in: Burnham, P. (ed.) *Surviving the Research Process in Politics,* London and Washington, Pinter.

Burnham, P. (ed.) (1997) *Surviving the Research Process in Politics,* London/Washington: Pinter.

Cowen, R. (1999) 'Comparative Perspectives on the British PhD', in: Graves, N. & Varma, V. (eds.) *Working for a Doctorate. A Guide for the Humanities and Social Sciences,* London and New York, Routledge.

Delamont, S., Atkinson, P. and Parry, O. (1999) *Supervising the PhD. A Guide to Success,* Buckingham/Philadelphia, SRHE and Open University Press.

Deutsch, K. (1957) *Political Community and the North Atlantic Area,* Princeton, Princeton University Press.

Dogan, M. (2000) 'Political Science and the Other Social Sciences' in: Goodin, R. E. and Klingemann, H-D. *A New Handbook of Political Science,* Oxford: Oxford University Press.

Engerman, S. L. (2000) 'Max Weber as Economist and Economic Historian', in: Turner, S. (ed.) *The Cambridge Companion to Weber,* Cambridge, Cambridge University Press.

ESRC (Economic and Social Research Council) (2001) *Postgraduate Training Guidelines,* 3rd edition.

Fairbairn, G. J. and Winch, C. (2000) *Reading, Writing and Reasoning. A Guide for Students,* Buckingham/Philadelphia, Open University Press, 2nd edition.

Frankfort-Nachmias, C. and Nachmias, D. (1992) *Research Methods in the Social Sciences,* London, Edward Arnold, 4th edition.

Geertz, C. (1973) *The Interpretation of Cultures,* New York, Basic Books.

Goodin, R. E. and Klingemann, H-D. (2000) *A New Handbook of Political Science,* Oxford, Oxford University Press.

Grant, W. (2000) 'Elite Interviewing: A Practical Guide', Institute for German Studies, Birmingham University, Discussion Paper, No.11.

Graves, N. (1999) 'Problems of Supervision', in: Graves, N. and Varma, V. (eds.) *Working for a Doctorate. A Guide for the Humanities and Social Sciences,* London/New York, Routledge.

Graves, N. and Varma, V. (eds.) (1999) *Working for a Doctorate. A Guide for the Humanities and Social Sciences,* London/New York, Routledge.

Grix, J. (2000) *The Role of the Masses in the Collapse of the GDR,* Basingstoke, Macmillan.

Grix, J. (2001) 'Social Capital as a Concept in the Social Sciences: the Current State of the Debate', *Democratization,* 8(3): 189-210.

The Guardian (2001), 'MIT to put its courses free on the internet', 6 April.

Hart, C. (2000) *Doing a Literature Review,* London, Sage.

Hartley, J. (1999) 'Writing the Thesis', in: Graves, N. and Varma, V. (eds.) *Working for a Doctorate: A Guide for the Humanities and Social Sciences,* London/New York, Routledge.

Hay, C. (1995) 'Structure and Agency', in: Marsh, D. and Stoker, G. (eds.) *Theory and Methods in Political Science,* Basingstoke, Macmillan.

Hay, C. (2002) *Political Analysis,* Basingstoke, Palgrave, manuscript.

Hirschman, A. O. (1970) *Exit, Voice, and Loyalty. Responses to Decline in Firms, Organizations, and States,* Cambridge, MA/London, Harvard University Press.

Hoffman, A. and Knowles, V. (1999) 'Germany and the Reshaping of Europe. Identifying Interests – The Role of Discourse Analysis', ESRC-IGS Working Paper No. 9.

Holloway, I. (1997) *Basic Concepts for Qualitative Research,* Oxford, Blackwell Science.

Honderich, T. (ed.) (2001) *The Philosophers. Introducing Great Western Thinkers,* Oxford, Oxford University Press.

Hutton, W. (1996) *The State We're In,* London, Vintage.

Hutton, W. (1999) *The Stakeholding Society, Writings on Politics and Economics,* Cambridge, Polity Press.

King, G., Keohane, O. and Verba, S. (1994) *Designing Social Inquiry. Scientific Inference in Qualitative Research,* Princeton, Princeton University Press.

Kuhn, T. S. (1996) *The Structure of Scientific Revolutions,* Chicago/London, University of Chicago Press.

Kumar, R. (1999) *Research Methodology. A Step-By-Step Guide for Beginners,* London/Thousand Oaks/New Delhi, Sage.

Landman, T. (2000) *Issues and Methods in Comparative Politics. An Introduction,* London/New York: Routledge.

Lewis-Beck. M. S. (1995) *Data Analysis: An Introduction,* London/Thousand Oaks/New Delhi, Sage.

Lawton, D. (1999) 'How to Succeed in Postgraduate Study', in: *Working for A Doctorate: A Guide for the Humanities and Social Sciences,* London/New York, Routledge.

Lunt, N. and Davidson, C. (2000) 'Journey to the Centre of the (Academic) Universe: 20 Steps on Getting Published in Journals', *Politics* 20 (1): 43-50.

Marsh, D. and Stoker, G. (eds.) (1995) *Theory and Methods in Political Science,* Basingstoke, Macmillan.

May, D. (1999) 'Planning Time', in: Graves, N. and Varma, V. (eds.) (1999) *Working for a Doctorate. A Guide for the Humanities and Social Sciences,* London/New York, Routledge.

Merton, R. K. (1967) *On Theoretical Sociology,* New York, The Free Press.

Neuman, W. L. (2000) *Social Research Methods. Qualitative and Quantitative Approaches,* Boston, Allyn & Bacon, 4th edition.

Pennings, P., Keman, H. and Kleinnijenhuis, J. (1999) *Doing Research in Political Science. An Introduction to Comparative Methods and Statistics,* London/Thousand Oaks/New Delhi, Sage.

Peters, G. B. (1998) *Comparative Politics. Theory and Methods,* Basingstoke, Macmillan.

Phillips, E. M. and Pugh, D. S. (eds.) (1994) *How to Get a PhD. A Handbook for Students and their Supervisors,* Buckingham/Philadelphia, Open University Press.

Plato (1994) *Republic,* trans. Robin Wakefield, Oxford/New York, Oxford University Press.

Popper, K. (2000) *The Logic of Scientific Discovery*, London/New York, Routledge.

Punch, K. F. (2000a) *Developing Effective Research Proposals*, London/Thousand Oaks/New Delhi, Sage.

Punch, K. F. (2000b) *Introduction to Social Research. Quantitative and Qualitative Approaches*, London/Thousand Oaks/New Delhi, Sage.

Putnam, R. (1993) *Making Democracy Work. Civic Traditions in Modern Italy*, Princeton, Princeton University Press.

Putnam, R. (1996) 'The Strange Disappearance of Civic America', *The American Prospect*, 24 (Winter).

Putnam, R. (2000) *Bowling Alone: The Collapse and Revival of American Community*, New York, Simon & Schuster.

Ragin, C.C. (1994) *Constructing Social Research. The Unity and Diversity of Method*, Thousand Oaks: Pine Forge Press.

Ringer, F. (1997) *Max Weber's Methodology. The Unification of the Cultural and Social Sciences*, Cambridge/London, Harvard University Press.

Robins, G. S. (1995) 'Banking in a Transition Economy: East Germany After Unification', University of Oxford, unpublished PhD Thesis.

Robson, C. (1995) *Real World Research, A Resource for Social Scientists and Practitioner-Researchers*, Oxford/Cambridge MA, Blackwell.

Rosamond, B. (2000) *Theories of European Integration*, Basingstoke, Macmillan.

Rosamond, B. (2001) 'Plagiarism, Academic Norms and the Governance of the Profession', unpublished manuscript.

Rudestam, K. E. and Newton, R. R. (1992) *Surviving your Dissertation. A Comprehensive Guide to Content and Process*, London/Thousand Oaks/New Delhi, Sage.

Schnell, R., Hill, P. B. and Esser, E. (1999) *Methoden der empirischen Sozialforschung*, Munich/Vienna, R. Oldenbourg Press.

Silverman, D. (2000) *Doing Qualitative Research. A Practical Handbook*, London/Thousand Oaks/New Delhi, Sage.

Steiner, G. (1991) *Real Presences*, London/Boston, Faber & Faber.

Stoker, G. (1995) 'Introduction', in: Marsh, D. and Stoker, G. (eds.) *Theory and Methods in Political Science*, Basingstoke, Macmillan.

Turner, S. (ed.) (2000) *The Cambridge Companion to Weber*, Cambridge, Cambridge University Press.

Van Evera, S. (1997) *Guide to Methods for Students of Political Science*, Ithaca, NY/London: Cornell University Press.

Vickers, R. (1997) 'Using Archives in Political Research', in: Burnham, P. (ed.) *Surviving the Research Process in Politics*, London/Washington, Pinter.

Weber, M. (1949) *The Methodology of the Social Sciences*, Trans. and ed. E. A. Shils and H. A. Finch, New York, Free Press.

Woolcock, M. (1998) 'Social Capital and Economic Development: Toward a Theoretical Synthesis and Policy Framework', *Theory and Society, Renewal and Critique in Social Theory*, 27(2): 151–208.

Yin, R. K. (1994) *Case Study Research. Design and Methods*, London/Thousand Oaks/New Delhi: Sage, 2nd edition.

Texts used for definitions of terms

Abercrombie, N., Hill, S. and Turner, B. S. (eds.) (1984) *The Penguin Dictionary of Sociology*, Harmondsworth, Penguin.

Encyclopedia Britannica, on-line version, www.britannica.com.

Klein, E. (1966 and 1967) *A Comprehensive Etymological Dictionary of the English Language*, Amsterdam/London/New York, Elsevier, vols I–III.

Simpson, J. A. and Weiner, E. S. C. (1989) *The Oxford English Dictionary*, Oxford, Clarendon Press, 2nd edition.

Wehmeier, S. (ed.) (2000) *Oxford Advanced Learner's Dictionary*, Oxford, Oxford University Press.

Index

Note: page numbers in **bold** refer to definitions of important terms.